OUT OF THE PAST
The Istanbul Grand Bazaar

For Melanie
with love —
An oldie — but a goodie
with love,
from Charlotte

OUT OF THE PAST
The Istanbul Grand Bazaar

Burton Y. Berry

Sketches and Jacket Illustration
by Azzedine el-Aaji

ARCO PUBLISHING COMPANY INC.
219 Park Avenue South, New York, N.Y. 10003

To Dr. Herman B Wells,

a friend since college days, whose dedication
to advancing the interests of Indiana University
roughly paralleled in time my saga of the
Istanbul Grand Bazaar.

Published by Arco Publishing Company, Inc.
219 Park Avenue South, New York, N.Y. 10003

Copyright © 1977 by Arco Publishing Company

All rights reserved. No part of this book may be reproduced,
in any form, by any means, without permission in writing
from the publisher.

Library of Congress Cataloging in Publication Data

Berry, Burton Yost.
    Out of the past: The Istanbul grand bazaar.

    1. Berry, Burton Yost—Art collections.
2. Istanbul. Kapalıçarşi. 3. Diplomats—United
States—Correspondence, reminiscences, etc.
I. Title.

N5220.B46A52   704.'7[B]   74-29791
ISBN 0-668-03778-4 (Cloth Edition)

Printed in the United States of America

Contents

Preface		7
Plates		9
Chapter I:	**Embroideries**	19
Plates		33
Chapter II:	**The Grand Bazaar**	47
Plates		59
Chapter III:	**Rugs, Carpets, Brocades, and Velvets**	71
Plates		79
Chapter IV:	**Old Silver**	89
Plates		95
Chapter V:	**Bronzes**	103
Plates		111
Chapter VI:	**Gem Stones and Jewelry**	117
Plates		127
Chapter VII:	**Byzantine Solidi**	137
Plates		145
Chapter VIII:	**Ancient Greek Coins**	155
Plates		171

Preface

In 1928 I first saw Istanbul, or Constantinople as the city was then usually called. I fell in love with the place at first sight. The people were kindly disposed, and all that I saw was different and exciting and enchanting to a young fellow fresh from rural Indiana. On one of my first walking excursions into the city I visited the Grand Bazaar and was delighted. On entering any shop I was welcomed, then offered a small cup of freshly made Turkish coffee, or tea served in a little glass, and, instead of being pressured into buying, I was invited to feel at home, look around, and examine whatever appealed to me. The merchants were smiling and friendly and several of them in time became my close friends. Looking back to those glorious days of youth and discovery I have a fellow-feeling toward many of those merchants, some of whom prospered and retired, others went broke and disappeared, a few moved away, and, sadly, many more of the cherished friends of those days, including Mr. Harry Mandil, Turudu Osman Bey, and the young Merinsky, died long ago.

Why did "The Bazaar" appeal to me so strongly? Perhaps some of my childhood experiences may provide an explanation. I came from a frugal family. When an object had fulfilled its usefulness we cleaned it and then put it away in the attic. As a child it was always a delight to be allowed to play amid these treasures of other years and to create my own make-believe world around them. In our attic were the toys of my mother and grandmother; the wedding and other formal clothes of older generations; small scale models of farm machinery; the early Edison and Victor Victrola "talking machines"; the telephones from the private lines of my maternal grandfather of a time before there was a local public telephone exchange; photographs and paintings that had served their immediate purpose; and all manner of things that had once played an important role in our lives. The Bazaar, or more accurately that area of it that was devoted to the sale of "antiques," was in fact a huge attic where, in time, I was to uncover what were to me fabulous treasures with which to play. Perhaps that is the explanation of the Bazaar's attraction to me, or part of it, at least. Perhaps, too, as time went on, I enjoyed the thrill of knowing that through a gradually acquired expert's knowledge I could purchase a mundane object there at a price which, while satisfying the seller, was well under that which someone who "collected" such things would pay for the same thing. Whatever the explanation it was a fact that the Bazaar delighted me. It became a practice for me to visit it for a recreational hour or more each day after the American Consulate General, where I worked, closed. I even regretted that the Bazaar was closed on Sundays!

On these Bazaar excursions during my first assignment to Istanbul, from 1928-34, I was sometimes accompanied by a colleague, Vice Consul Raymond Hare, Robert English, or Howard Elting Jr., but most often by William Cramp, and occasionally by a friend, such as Betty Carp or Elsie Grew. When I was transferred to other posts and returned to the city on short holidays I went to the Bazaar alone. When I was reassigned to Istanbul in 1942 I made my daily pilgrimage frequently in the company of Consul William Fraleigh. After my retirement from the Foreign Service in 1954 I built a house on the hills overlooking the Bosphorus. Then I normally visited the Bazaar alone, or with Mr. Mahmud

Mehaydli. In the past year when I was checking the information for this book I was accompanied by Mr. Azzdine el-Aaji.

Some of the incidents recorded in the pages that follow I have lifted out of copies of correspondence with the late G. Howland Shaw, the friend of young people and one of the finest persons that I have ever known, and from that with Betty Carp, the staunch and loyal friend of most of my adult life. Other incidents were taken from notes that were made at the time but never used, and in certain chapters, such as those concerning gem stones and Greek coins, I have drawn heavily from my reading and from things that I have published. All that is reported actually happened, and, although on re-reading it today, some of the stories and language seem to have been taken straight out of the period of Harun al-Rashid, that was the mood of the place and people at the time that they were written.

In this account I hope to pass on to the reader some feeling of the atmosphere of the Istanbul Bazaar of forty years ago; an indication of what was available in the Bazaar at that and slightly later times, as well as some of the enjoyment that I experienced in visiting the Bazaar, all held together by the thread of my personal experiences. I wish, too, to record the respect and friendship that I felt, then and now, for the persons I have named.

Finally, I wish to add a word of caution for enthusiastic new collectors against interpreting this book as an invitation to visit Turkey with the hope of finding and carrying away treasures of great value that were picked up at little cost in the Grand Bazaar. True, a recommendation to visit Turkey is implicit in every line, and the Grand Bazaar of Istanbul remains an enchanting place. But the visitor today should always bear in mind that the Bazaar merchants are well informed of the world prices of what they offer for sale, and that a new antiquities law, published in 1973, prohibits the exportation of objects enumerated in the law.

Burton Y. Berry

Cairo, Egypt
January 18, 1974

Plates for the Preface

		Page
1.	The route of most of today's tourists to the Bazaar is through the courtyard of the Nuri Osmaniye mosque. (BYB-1973.)	11
2.	Crowds of people entering and leaving the Bazaar via Mahmud Pasha Street on an autumn afternoon just before a holiday. (BYB-1973.)	12
3.	The outer courtyard of the mosque of Sultan Bayazid II. (BYB-1956.)	13
4.	The street of the booksellers leading from the mosque of Sultan Bayazid II to the western entrances of the Bazaar. (BYB-1929.)	14
5.	Two Bazaar merchants passing their time between visits of customers with a game of backgammon. (BYB-1972.)	15
6.	Although there is nearly seventy years difference in age, both are Bazaar habitués. (BYB-1972.)	16

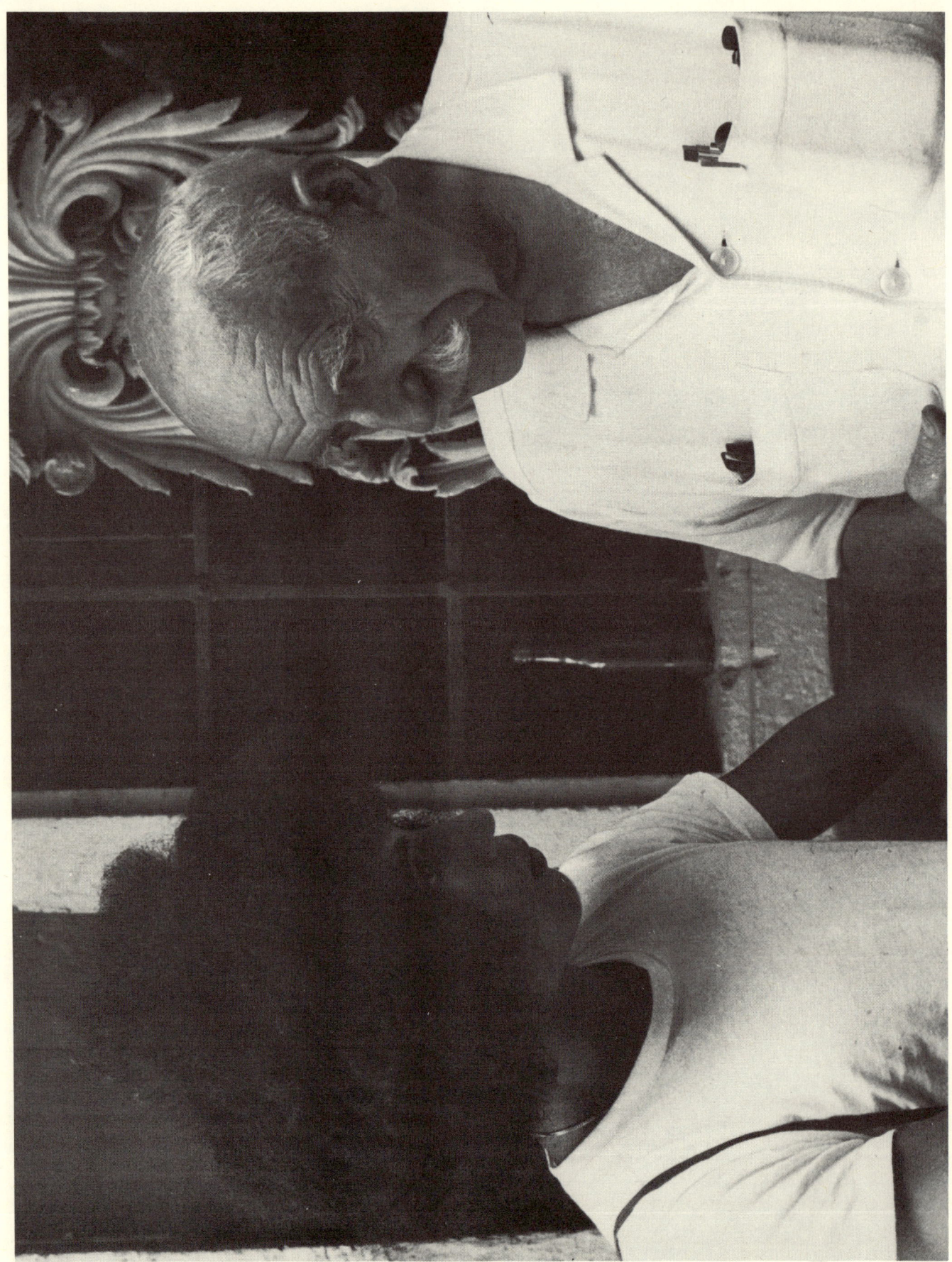

OUT OF THE PAST
The Istanbul Grand Bazaar

I
Embroideries

Everybody in the Istanbul diplomatic community in 1928 collected something, or at least said that they collected something, for, I was later to learn, some of those who talked the most about their collections actually had the least. Almost everybody did visit the Bazaar more or less regularly and so what one saw, or "found," or "lost," or bought in the Bazaar was very often the opening subject of a conversation when foreigners met.

Thus, for me, a newly arrived member of the local community, a problem gradually emerged. "What did I collect?" I liked some of the beautiful rugs that I saw in the Bazaar, but they were too expensive for me to buy. I admired the ancient weapons, jewelled daggers with gold incrusted damascened blades, and the fantastically shaped and decorated firearms, but they sometimes cost even more than the rugs. I thought a lot about the problem but had no ready answer, which, when it did surface, came quite unexpectedly.

While sitting with me one afternoon Turudu Osman Bey, who with his three brothers were often spoken of affectionately, but quite inaccurately, as "the four Macedonian bandits," because they had come from Saloniki in Macedonia, pulled out of a bale of rags a very beautiful fragment of something or other. I asked what it was. Osman shrugged his shoulders and said that it was probably a piece from one end of an old Turkish towel. Since his attitude indicated that it was not worth much money, I asked the price, and as it was really very little, I bought it.

I showed my purchase to Mr. Harry Mandil who enthusiastically confirmed my opinion of its beauty and antiquity, adding that it was really a bargain. Thereupon I decided to keep an eye open for other such fragments. The same evening I showed my prize to Vice Consul William Cramp, my friend whose keen judgment was usually hidden behind a quip. "Ah!" he said with a deep sigh, "a problem of the American community is finally solved. You will henceforth be tagged as a buyer of discarded Turkish towels." And so, with a raised eyebrow, or other deprecating gesture, he spread the word to our mutual secret delight. The looks of anguish, disgust, and even horror on the faces of our more conventional colleagues, and their wives, when they first got the message, was really something to remember. "Did you hear," I recall Bill Cramp once saying to a lady at a party in a stage whisper loud enough for me to overhear, "today Berry bought from a rag-picker a towel six inches wide and fourteen feet long, terribly stained. What could those stains be?" The lady recoiled as though the "terribly stained" cloth had been pushed violently into her hands, and then Cramp went on to continue his missionary work with someone else, who, as Cramp talked, usually gave me a quick glance over the shoulder and then half-turned away as if to avoid contamination. We kept a record of how many times Cramp scored at each party; he even invented a scale on which he noted the degree of shock registered.

And so my "collection" began as a joke which we really enjoyed. But I was soon to pay for my fun as it was not long before some of the more aggressive ladies asked to see my collection. Cramp sometimes assisted at the showings, eloquently providing most of the horror stories. This, too, was fun, but also it was expensive as the visitor too often asked a tangible souvenir of her visit in the form of a towel! For a

Embroidered detail from the border of an eighteenth-century bed covering. Aegean Islands.

while I consoled myself that I had had my fun, and that my guest, convinced of the pleasures of towel collecting, had carried away her own problem as to how to continue to be a member in good standing of a scoffing community while at the same time preserving her own self-respect by admitting the beauty, and the possession, of a towel. It was amusing to observe how this was accomplished, the usual mental gymnastics being to place the fault on the collector, while holding the object collected in high regard—since she now had acquired an example! But in spite of the favors that came my way, I felt that I was overpaying, and in the Bazaar community this is *the* mortal sin. So Cramp and I decided that henceforth I was to be the "student" engrossed in research, and preparing to publish something truly profound on "The Towel," and that in the meantime I should not talk about towels, or show my collection, even though he hinted to the inquisitive ladies that it was becoming truly fabulous. It must be admitted that our decision was influenced by the need of appearing as acceptable subordinates in the eyes of the Consul in Istanbul and the Washington bureaucracy, for then acceptable meant being conventional.

Little did I think, at the time, that I was moving more deeply into a trap, for we failed to realize the tenacity of the ladies when refused their rights, as they saw them, and the strength of the attraction for the unusual. The ladies continued to inquire more and more persistently about my researches, asking if I had started to publish them, or when I expected to start publishing them, or where I kept my treasures now that they had become too valuable to keep in my apartment. In a desperate effort to preserve my privacy and keep my collection safe from depredators I wrote to Miss Julie Michelet, Curator of Textiles at the Art Institute of Chicago:

Dear Miss Michelet:

I am forced to do something in self-defense and for the reason that every few days somebody turns up and asks to see my collection of towels. I ask them to my house for tea and then bring out a few examples. They gasp more or less naturally and then, when they have recovered their voices, say "You MUST, Mr. Berry, tell us ALL about them." And I tell them a few facts! While this ritual was very good fun for the first dozen times, it became rather dreary for me and finally downright boring. So, as you can imagine, I have been looking for ways of escape. Since "working" and "studying" only serve to postpone my tea parties I must find a strong excuse to stop the requests. It occurred to me that I could offer to loan the Chicago Art Institute a half a dozen towels for two or three years. Then I could greet all comers with a polite "So sorry, but you know that I have loaned my best pieces to the Art Institute of Chicago, and the

Embroidered flower spray from a seventeenth-century Turkish towel.

others, well . . . ." So if you have a spare shelf or two in a case and would like to cover that shelf with towels, please drop me a line and I shall bring a half a dozen pieces to America when I depart for the States on my leave next month.

Very sincerely,

Istanbul, Turkey
August 9, 1932

    Miss Michelet replied enthusiastically and I sent eight towels to Chicago in 1932. They formed a part of the Art Institute's show during the Century of Progress Exposition in Chicago, and Miss Helen Gunsaulus, Miss Michelet's successor, wrote me after the Exposition closed, that by count more than a million people had passed through the galleries during the period, and many of them had expressed pleasure and surprise on first seeing the old Turkish towels. With this encouragement I gradually increased my loan, later to become a gift, until it exceeded four hundred specimens. And, in Istanbul, because of the resulting publicity, I was able to say to the local ladies, "You must plan a trip to Chicago. Go at once before it is too late!" Indeed, some of them did visit Chicago and see the towels on their holidays at home! But this only served to increase the inquiries about my research and my writings, and in the end I was forced to do both as the only way out of an impossible situation. At that time I regretted that Bill Cramp was no longer beside me. He had been transferred to Belize, British Honduras, as a punishment, he thought, for his unconventionality while working in Istanbul.

    One afternoon after I had come from a visit to the Old Palace of the Sultans, I sat in the Bazaar with Turudu Osman Bey, and talked with him about the treasures that I had seen there. He asked if I knew how the Sultans chose their wives and concubines. Then he went on to say that a Sultan usually had four

Embroidered "kiosk and cypress" motif from an eighteenth-century Turkish towel.

official wives and as many concubines as he wished. The candidates were screened by his mother, the Valide Sultan, who at an appropriate time assembled the girls in a row in her audience chamber in the Palace Harem. The Sultan paid a visit to his mother then walked slowly down the line and on his return placed a beautifully embroidered towel on the shoulders of the girl of his choice. The story was certainly romantic, Oriental, and entirely fitting to the place, but I asked how the embroidered towel also fit into a masculine world, as he had once told me it did. Osman said that today he would give one example, and later others. Then he related that at the time of the Bayram feast it used to be the custom for the Sultan and the men of his Court to go to the Plain of Kagithane on the Golden Horn and to engage in contests of distance and accuracy shooting with their long bows and arrows. The prize of victory was invariably an embroidered towel. Indeed, today, he said, there still exist stone shafts in the Kagithane meadow upon which are engraved records of these tournaments. I went to Kagithane later and saw some of the shafts, confirming thereby that Osman's Bazaar stories were often historically correct.

In 1930, an American tourist in Istanbul asked me "What is a Turkish towel?" I was hard put to find a simple answer in spite of the fact that I had examined more than 16,000 towels in the Istanbul Bazaar during the two previous years. Admittedly the word *towel* is an inaccuracy, but in time it has become accepted, at least in the Oriental markets, as the word to describe a strip of cotton or linen material ornamented at each end by an embroidered motif.

Embroidery is a minor art. It is a domestic art. Towels were the most numerous products of this art, but they were generally less highly regarded by the local people than the larger and richer products, such as wall hangings, curtains, prayer rugs, bed sheets, and pillow covers. These grander examples of the embroiderer's art were made mostly for the ornamentation of palaces and religious buildings. The walls of the Kaaba at Mecca, for example, as well as many other sacred buildings, were once covered with embroideries but because of the perishable quality of the material, they were, for the most part, ultimately removed and often replaced by carved stone and painted faience imitating the embroideries. Mr. Thomas Whittemore, the man who in our time first received permission to uncover the Byzantine mosaics of St. Sophia, once remarked as we looked at some late faience tile paneling in a mosque, "And the next step is linoleum." His remark seemed almost sacrilegious to me, but I had to admit to myself that the repeated stamped patterns on the tiles, although inspired by textiles, had lost something of their freshness and beauty in the transition. However, such embroideries continued to be made, and can still be seen in mosques used as curtains for the mimbar, or covers for especially prized Korans written by famous calligraphers. Later I was to acquire some of these, but the towels, being personal, relatively small, very beautiful, immensely varied in design, and comparatively inexpensive, have always appealed to me more than the larger embroideries. Even Mr. Whittemore regarded them with favor for they were "of the people." Another reason for my concentration on towels was that in Istanbul I had the market largely to myself, whereas the more important embroideries had many ready purchasers in discriminating and wealthy amateurs, such as Mrs. Helen Stathatou and Mr. Anthony Benaki of Athens; Mrs. McCormick of Chicago; Mrs. Hannaux of Cairo; Mr. J. Soustiel of Paris; Mrs. Frank Cook; Professor R. M. Dawkins; and Mr. A. J. B. Wace of England. Sometime later the interest of Mr. Kazim Taskent, the able and energetic director of the Yapi ve Kredi Bank, was aroused by the towels and he formed a fine collection for the Bank.

The descriptions of towels in the old travel books and diaries of European visitors to the Near East lack precision. Often I came across the phrase "embroidered in silks and gold in the finest manner" describing a towel. Contemporaneous Turkish writers left few exact records of towels. European painters of Turkish scenes generally ignored textiles, with the one exception of Holbein whose paintings carefully depicted Turkish rugs. Oriental miniaturists, because of the smallness of their medium, could only indicate the presence of embroideries and give an impression of their beauty. I soon learned that I could get very little information about the towels that I saw in the Bazaar from the libraries and museums.

In the Bazaar through observation, listening, and patience I did learn quite a bit. And now, to avoid the error of the enthusiastic foreign visitors to Turkey in other centuries, I wish to record some facts about towels. First, for the physical aspects: Towels vary in width from nine to forty-two inches and in length from two to fourteen feet. The embroidered band at each end is from two to twenty inches wide. The embroidery is practically identical on each side. The toweling may be linen or cotton and the embroidery is normally in colored silk, metal, or tinsel, or a combination of all of these. The towels were made to be used as kerchiefs, veils, belts, wrappers for precious objects, handkerchiefs, napkins, or towels. Whatever their purpose, they were all made for personal use. In the course of time I learned that these Turkish embroideries were not only made by Turks but also by Armenians, Greeks, and other minorities living within the territory of the Ottoman Empire.

A seventeenth century towel, the oldest that I was to find in the Bazaar, was from four to six feet long and eighteen to twenty-four inches wide. The toweling was generally linen, coarsely woven with up to twenty threads to the lineal inch. There was no woven design in the toweling. The embroidery was a band across each end. The eighteenth century towels of the best quality were made of very fine cotton toweling woven in a long strip and cut in the length desired. The loom width varied between twenty-two and twenty-seven inches. There can be as many as fifty threads to a lineal inch on some towels. It is this stuff that incited the romantic comments of travellers, as "the material is only one degree coarser than steam vapor." In the nineteenth century towel sizes tended to be standardized into two sizes which in America we would call "hand towels" and "bath towels." Both were of cotton. The bath towel, and it was really made to be used as a wrapper in leaving the Turkish bath, was woven in a looped stitch that abroad is identified as "Turkish toweling."

In the seventeenth century the usual medium of embroidery was a loosely twisted silk thread dyed red, blue, or black. The dyes were made from the plant life growing close at hand; the red was from madder root, the blue from any of the indigofera plants, and the black from the acorns of the Valonia oak. Yellow was also used in the seventeenth century. It came from the daphne plant. Green was of course a combination of yellow and blue. In Turkey, purple came from the blackberry fruit.

As the vegetable black was not a fast color and faded to brown quickly, a mineral dye, made by dissolving scraps of iron in acid, was often used. This produced a strong color but in time it rotted the thread. Thus, the original black edging of seventeenth century towels disappeared entirely or remained as brown, either one to the disadvantage of the embroidery. Unfortunately no general solution was found for the problem until the introduction into Turkey from Europe of commercially manufactured dyes. I passed many happy hours discussing local dyes with Bay Tahsin Oz, assistant and later Curator of the Seraglio Museum in Istanbul. Tahsin Bey had a passion for Turkish textiles and was always on the alert to preserve the best of them for the National collection. At the same time he was a generous man who was quick to help a private collector with his knowledge, often indicating to me where I could buy a choice piece that was not desired for the museum.

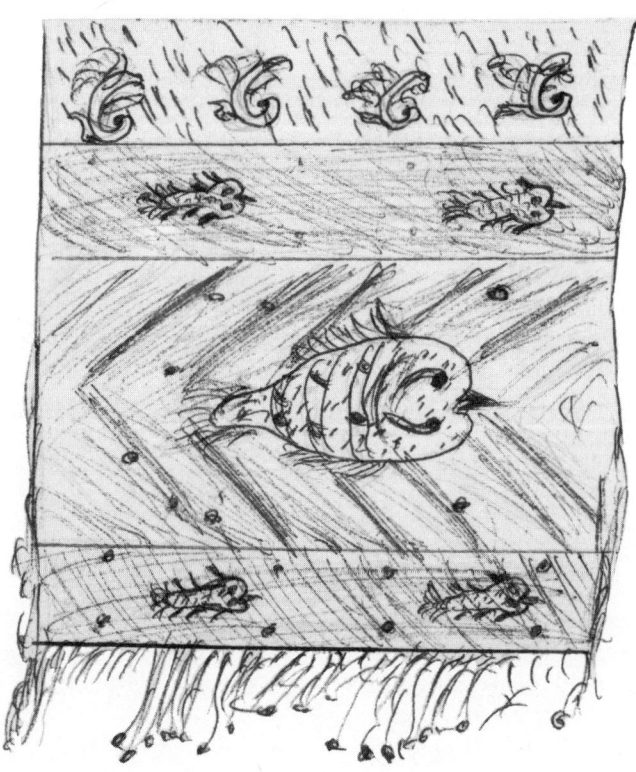

An example from an eighteenth-century Turkish towel of silver tinsel and green silk thread being used to make a mesh-like embroidered background. The motif is of fish swimming.

Very occasionally I did see a towel where the design had been edged with a lustrous black filament and, using a magnifying glass, saw that this filament was human hair. I never saw hair other than black used as an embroidery medium on an embroidery from Turkey, and, since many local people are blond, and some even redheaded, I suppose that the black hair, when used, was used as a substitute after failing to obtain a satisfactory black color for silk or cotton threads from vegetable dyes. Miss Christine Papadopoulo, a descendant of a local Greek family, once gave me an embroidery made entirely of human hair telling me that it had been made in 1745 in Istanbul by Zoe Sofyanis, her great, great grandmother. Mrs. Alexander Vaglery gave me another piece which had been given to her by a member of an old Greek family from the Phanar. In the Bazaar, Elea, a Greek merchant, told me that using their own hair in embroidery had once been a sentimental practice of Greek maidens in building their dowries, or in making a gift to a betrothed. When I enquired, if such was a general practice in times past, why we never ran across such embroideries in the Bazaar, and especially in Greek shops such as his, he replied that such objects might be given away, or lost or even destroyed, but they would never be sold by the families that had made them.

In the eighteenth century silk thread, which had all the colors used in the previous century plus many new shades, was used in embroidery. Additionally tiny metal wires were twisted around a silk core and then used to enrich the embroidery. The wires were usually of silver washed in gold, so that they gave the appearance of gold. A metal tinsel made of thin strips of silver was sometimes also used in place of, or in addition to, metal thread. The silk thread was dyed in many secondary colors in addition to the original primary ones. In the nineteenth century every color known to Europe was used in Turkish embroideries.

A dish of pears. An embroidery motif from a nineteenth-century Turkish towel.

I was not much interested in the matter of stitchery, preferring to leave this subject to the professionals who, I soon found, disagreed violently among themselves in identifying and naming the types of stitches used. There was one exception to this. In the eighteenth century embroiderers began to enrich their work with very narrow strips of thin metal which, without the use of a needle, was passed through the toweling, then, over-passing several threads, passed back to a position near the starting

An elaborate scene, developed from the "kiosk and cypress" design, on a nineteenth-century Turkish towel.

Embroideries

point. The strip was pulled tight, drawing together the now hidden threads of the toweling, and completing the stitch with a knot. When an area of toweling is covered in this way it is transparent, metallic, and identical in appearance on either side. It is supple and has the general appearance of nylon window screening. I rather liked it and I was glad that Mr. Whittemore was not in Istanbul to make his comments when I bought my first towel decorated with this type of work!

The variation of the designs of the embroidery on Turkish towels is a source of never ending satisfaction to the collector. One of their charms is in their diversity. The oldest designs are ogival. They are of the sixteenth century. I never found such a towel in the Bazaar. In the seventeenth century a new style came into vogue. This was the floral spray. This innovation found a sympathetic reception from the nation and continued to be popular from the period of introduction until the beginning of the twentieth century when hand-woven and embroidered towels began to give way to the machine-made factory products. The floral motif changed and developed with time.

Originally it was a naturalistic spray consisting of a curved serrated leaf with a flower sheltering under it, and a stem with a hooked end. This unit was repeated sufficiently often to fill the space reserved for decoration at each end of the towel. The rose, the tulip, the carnation, and the hyacinth were the flowers most often depicted. As time passed the single flower spray evolved into an elaborate, sometimes multiple, spraylike confusion of flowers and leaves. Sometimes single sprays were united into a group by wavy bands, and sometimes by a series of arches, one over each spray. A variation of the flower spray often took the form of a dish of fruit. I have seen designs made of pears, apples, peaches, pomegranates, grapes, strawberries, and watermelons. Sometimes these designs were drawn and embroidered with great skill and precision, but more often they were pleasantly naive, even primitive, indicating the peasant source of the embroidery.

A rose-water flacon and an incense burner, embroidered designs from nineteenth-century Turkish towels.

In the eighteenth century the floral motif was sometimes expanded into a garden scene. Traditionally such a scene included a garden kiosk and a cypress tree or two, and is generally known as the "kiosk and cypress" design. Occasionally a very elaborate scene was developed with a rambling house on a hillside, which slopes to a stream of water, generally identified as the Bosphorus. All the space was filled with a profusion of flowers, shrubs, and trees. Sometimes birds are shown perched on the treetops or flying between the trees. Persons are rarely shown but, occasionally, in a doorway or window there is an indication of something that one can imagine is a person.

A dagger with verses from the Koran embroidered on the blade. A motif from a nineteenth-century Turkish towel.

Once in a while one comes across a towel where the embroidered band is entirely covered by verses from the Koran. This is really a talisman in the form of a towel, rather than a towel, and as such had little artistic interest for me. More frequently I saw towels ornamented with pictures of objects used in daily life for the entertainment of guests, such as the rose water flacon and the incense burner, which formerly were offered at meals after a guest had washed his hands, and dried them on an embroidered towel. The representations of sandals (rowboats), sailing caiques, and full-rigged vessels evoke thoughts of adventure and profit. When one meets a fish swimming in a golden sea he is intrigued as to whether the

A cock perched on a treetop. A motif from a nineteenth-century Turkish towel.

reference is to a recent pleasurable sporting event, or to a religious symbol first used by Christians living in an officially hostile Roman state and perhaps in later times by some timorous person living in a predominately Moslem community. Humor in embroidery always delights me. There is not as much of it on the Turkish towels as on the Greek embroideries of the same period, but there is enough to give pleasant variety. I enjoyed meeting, for example, the great cocks perched on treetops and the peacocks with flowering tails. The latter could be taken as the eighteenth century reincarnation of the grylloi on

Embroideries

some Roman intaglios found in Anatolia. And if not exactly humor, I enjoyed the clear message of a towel, sent as a gift to some perfidious individual, decorated with daggers on which are inscribed verses from the Koran exhorting the living of a proper life!

A peacock with a flowering tail. A motif from a nineteenth-century Turkish towel.

While searching for towels and information about them, I recall Mr. Michel Akaoui once showing me a very unusual piece featuring stylized dragons. I asked him about the significance of the motif. He said that he did not know but that I might get a clue by looking at ancient manuscripts. Mr. Akaoui had been educated to become a Roman Catholic priest, and would have been, except for the sudden death of a relative, a Bazaar merchant. He had a responsibility, too, for his sister's minor children. In the tradition of the city there was nothing for Mr. Akaoui to do but to renounce his own career, take over the business of his deceased relative, and act as the head of the family educating his nephews. In view of his seminary training his suggestion to me had more than ordinary merit, and because of this and with the help of friendly librarians and museum curators, I was able to examine many ancient manuscripts illustrated with miniatures which had formed a part of the old Imperial libraries. When I went on holiday abroad I went through the Chester Beatty collection of manuscripts, and other private and public collections, seeking information. The gleanings were meager, but the experience was broadening and pleasurable. I came back from each of these academic excursions with a sharpened interest for work in my laboratory—the Bazaar of Istanbul.

Mr. Akaoui's reference to old manuscripts makes me remember a thought of Helen Gunsaulus who wrote (in the Bulletin of the Art Institute of Chicago in February, 1934):

"The towels or scarves (of Mr. Berry's collection) are embroidered on very soft tissue-like homespun cotton. The stitchery is extremely fine, both sides being practically identical. The patterns are so lavish in their colored silks and metal threads that one wonders that the embroiderers could work on such a thin foundation.... The soft colors, the tiny glints of gold, the tones of ivory of an old towel remind one of an illuminated manuscript."

The rapid expansion of the Ottoman Empire began in the fifteenth century with Mehmet I, who offered asylum and encouragement to the artists driven from their homes in the East by civil wars. The expansion, continued by the capture of Constantinople in 1453 by Mehmet II, brought great wealth and widened cultural experiences to the Osmanlis. As these Sultans and their successors went from military victory to victory, adding provinces to the Empire, wealth flowed into the capital and the taste for luxuries increased. This tendency continued through the fifteenth, sixteenth, and seventeenth centuries.

A variation of the "kiosk and cypress" design from an eighteenth-century Turkish towel.

Another variation of the "kiosk and cypress" design from an eighteenth-century Turkish towel.

Even a setback such as the crushing defeat of the Turkish fleet at Lepanto in 1571 caused only a minor shock and hardly affected the extravagances of the ruling families. On that occasion the Grand Vizier, the Sultan's first minister, is reported to have said to the Grand Admiral Kilij Ali Pasha when he questioned the financial ability of the Empire to build a new Turkish fleet, "Lord Admiral, the wealth and power of the Empire are such that if it is necessary we would make anchors of silver, cables of silk, and sails of satin." Even after the Turkish retreat from the gates of Vienna in 1683, the riches of the capital were so great and the tradition of luxury so well established that the expensive ways of living gave way reluctantly before the forces of economic necessity. The ornamentation of textiles, in weaving and embroidery, generally paralleled this historic development, although there was obviously a time lag between the greatest victories and the greatest art—it takes longer to build than to destroy. There was a corresponding, but perhaps shorter, lag between the time of decline of the fortunes of the Empire and the decadence of artistic development as evidenced in the textiles.

Sometimes I was asked where the towels that appeared in the Istanbul Bazaar came from. At the time that I was working on them they came mostly from Anatolia. They were brought to the city by itinerant peddlers who went from village to village selling yard goods and taking payment in cash or anything that they could resell at a profit in the city. Each of these men had his own territory in which he moved about in a continuous circuit. In coming to Istanbul each sold his harvest to Osman Bey, or one of the few other wholesalers, who in turn supplied the principal antique dealers with selected pieces. After I had learned the procedure I arranged with Osman, and the others, for them to keep their purchases intact in the bales in which they arrived until I could see them. I promised that if I were the first to look through the bales I would visit the Bazaar every afternoon and would surely find something to buy. Under this plan I was able to see the merchandise as it reached the market and I hoped that this would help me to isolate patterns by area. I kept careful charts during the winters of 1928 and 1929 but the results of my work were largely negative. I concluded that motifs were simply styles that had caught on in one locality and not in another. The motifs were rarely subjects of local tradition. In fact, after cataloguing some 16,000 old towels on their arrival in Istanbul about the only statement that I would make concerning provenance with any degree of certainty was that fine work and wealth were never very far apart. But Osman, more out of friendship than the hope of financial gain, did his best for me and the peddlers cooperated. Osman encouraged them to talk freely and I learned where they bought each important piece, and often the circumstance surrounding the purchase was interesting. Occasionally when a design on a towel intrigued me particularly, the peddler from whom I got it would bring some information about it to me on a later trip. In all this Osman was constantly helpful as a friend and a catalyst, with the result that I saw practically every bale of textiles that reached Istanbul from the country. In examining them I

Still another variation of the "kiosk and cypress" design from an eighteenth-century Turkish towel.

must have breathed countless microbes, but, nonetheless, I kept amazingly healthy, perhaps aided by the exercise I got in walking to and from the Bazaar, and from my frugal supper of country yogurt and fresh Turkish bread—the tastiest that I know—which saved me extra cash for my Bazaar forays.

Once, while traveling in Anatolia, I bought a beautifully embroidered eighteenth century towel in Merzifon. The material was of the finest and the embroidery of the best. Surprised to have found such a lovely piece in such a remote place, I asked the merchant from whom I had made my purchase for the name of the former owner. He referred me to a locally prominent family. Friends of mine knew them and so it was arranged that I call on them. In the course of the meeting I learned that the towel had been family property for as long as any member of the family could remember. I also learned that the family in Merzifon dated back about one hundred and fifty years, when one of the forebears had been exiled there.

One more variation of the "kiosk and cypress" design from an eighteenth-century Turkish towel.

My host did not say so, but it is my opinion that the towel which I had purchased was brought to Merzifon from Istanbul with the household of the exiled family. That is, I think, a likely explanation of finding this, and many another, beautiful piece of Turkish embroidery in an out-of-the-way corner of the country.

In 1931 I wrote, "The Turkish eighteenth century embroidered towels are the most beautiful embroideries made in the Near East. Although they have always been collected and esteemed at home and abroad, the available supply of them is sufficiently large for representative collections to be assembled today. They are found in the homes of the rich and of the poor throughout Turkey and to a lesser extent in the homes of the people of the hereditary states of the Ottoman Empire. There are some fine private collections in Europe and America, and examples are to be seen in the great museums of both continents. They can be bought today in the Bazaars of Istanbul and Cairo, and in the antique shops of Athens, London, and Paris..." In re-reading this forty years later I thought, that while the collections in the museums may have remained intact, most of the private collections have been dispersed by the heirs of the collectors, the towels once in the homes of the people have disappeared under waves of modernization, and it has been many a year since I have seen a first-class towel offered for sale in the Bazaars and antique shops. So greatly do conditions change in a relatively short time! I continued my reverie recalling that as the supply of towels had decreased, public interest slackened until eventually both all but disappeared. My own interest and research, which at one time had caused tongues to wag excitedly, had ended in a great void of silence. I had published a report on towels in 1932 in the *Art Bulletin*, the publication of the American College Art Association, and another in 1938. I had written in other American and English publications. I had lectured in several countries. My collection had had three major showings in Chicago, each for several months, one of them occupying three galleries during the showing. Considerably more than a million people had visited those galleries for one showing. The collection was catalogued in a splendidly illustrated and sympathetically written publication by Margaret Gentles, the third Keeper of Textiles at the Art Institute of Chicago, who had cared for the

A sailing caïque. A motif from an eighteenth-century Turkish towel.

A full-rigged vessel. A motif from an eighteenth-century Turkish towel.

A large sandal, or rowboat, with auxiliary sail. A motif from an eighteenth-century Turkish towel.

collection with loving hands. The project had matured to an unusually rich and full ending but nobody was really looking, and that included me. There was no cause for sadness as the air of the Bazaar is charged with excitement and hope. One interest may die but another is born—and that birth may be twins!

Plates for Chapter I

All objects are in the Art Institute of Chicago. (Photographs courtesy of the Art Institute.)

		Page
7.	Sixteenth-century Turkish cover. The design is of pomegranate fruits and leaves attached to curving stems. The colors are red and green.	35
8.	Seventeenth-century Turkish hanging. The lines of the ogival pattern are brought together at regular intervals by a crown and enclose an artichoke surrounded by serrated leaf forms. The colors are red, blue, green, white, and black.	36
9.	Seventeenth-century bedspread from Yannina, Epirus. This embroidery surfaced in the Istanbul Bazaar and was used by the buyer as a throw over a screen in his Athens apartment. The colors are red, blue, green, yellow, white, and black. The table cover is a fragment of a sixteenth-century Bursa velvet. A seventeenth-century dragon Kuba rug is on the floor. (BYB-1937.)	37
10.	Seventeenth-century bedspread from the Ionian Islands. The motif is a marriage scene supported by abundant trees, flowers, and birds. The colors are red, blue, yellow, green, white and black.	38
11.	Eighteenth-century Turkish turban scarf. The design is a repeated rose spray. The colors are red, yellow, blue, black, and white.	39
	Fragment of a seventeenth-century Turkish hanging. The design is composed of tulips and artichokes. The colors are red, blue, and green.	
12.	An eighteenth-century picture. The work is embroidered entirely in human hair.	40
13.	Seventeenth-century Turkish towel ends. The design is a repeated rose spray. The colors are red, blue, green, white, and black.	41
	Seventeenth-century Turkish towel ends. The design is a repeated rose spray. The colors are red, blue, green, white, and black.	
14.	The ends of an eighteenth-century Turkish towel. The design is an elaborate repeated rose spray. The colors are gold, red, blue, yellow, green, and brown all in several shades, plus gold and silver metal threads.	42
15.	The ends of an eighteenth-century Turkish towel. The design is a repeated rose spray held together by serrated leaves. The colors are red, blue, yellow, and green, all in several shades, and gold and silver.	43
	The ends of an eighteenth to nineteenth-century Turkish towel. The design is a repeated rose spray held together by floral arches. The colors are gold, red, blue, yellow, green, and brown in several shades.	
16.	The end of an eighteenth-century Turkish towel. The design is a scene of houses and gardens beside a stream of water, possibly the Bosphorus. The colors are gold, red, blue, yellow, green, and brown.	44

Embroideries

		Page
	The end of an eighteenth-century Turkish towel. The design is of repeated cypress and beech trees and garden kiosks. The colors are blue, green, brown, and purple.	
17.	One end each from three nineteenth-century Turkish towels.	45
	A dish of pears or figs. The colors are gold, white, red, green, and blue.	
	Rose water sprinklers and incense burners. The colors are gold, red, green, white, and black.	
	Peacocks with flowering tails. The colors are gold, red, blue, green, and black.	
18.	The end of a nineteenth-century Turkish towel. The design is a great tree with tents beneath, repeated. The colors are gold, black, and shades of green.	46
	The end of a nineteenth-century Turkish towel. The design is a repeated rose spray. The colors are gold, red, green, and black.	

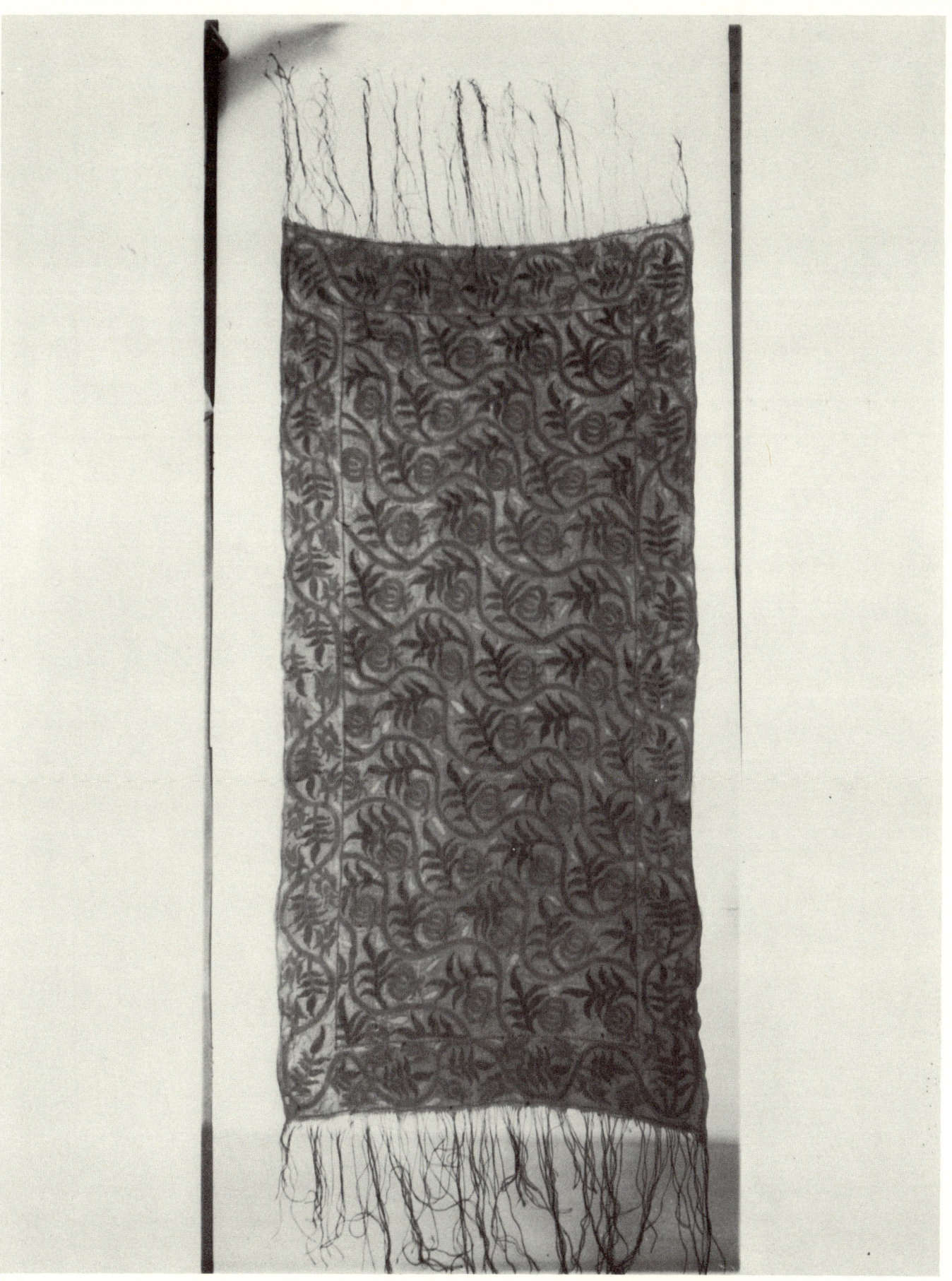

38

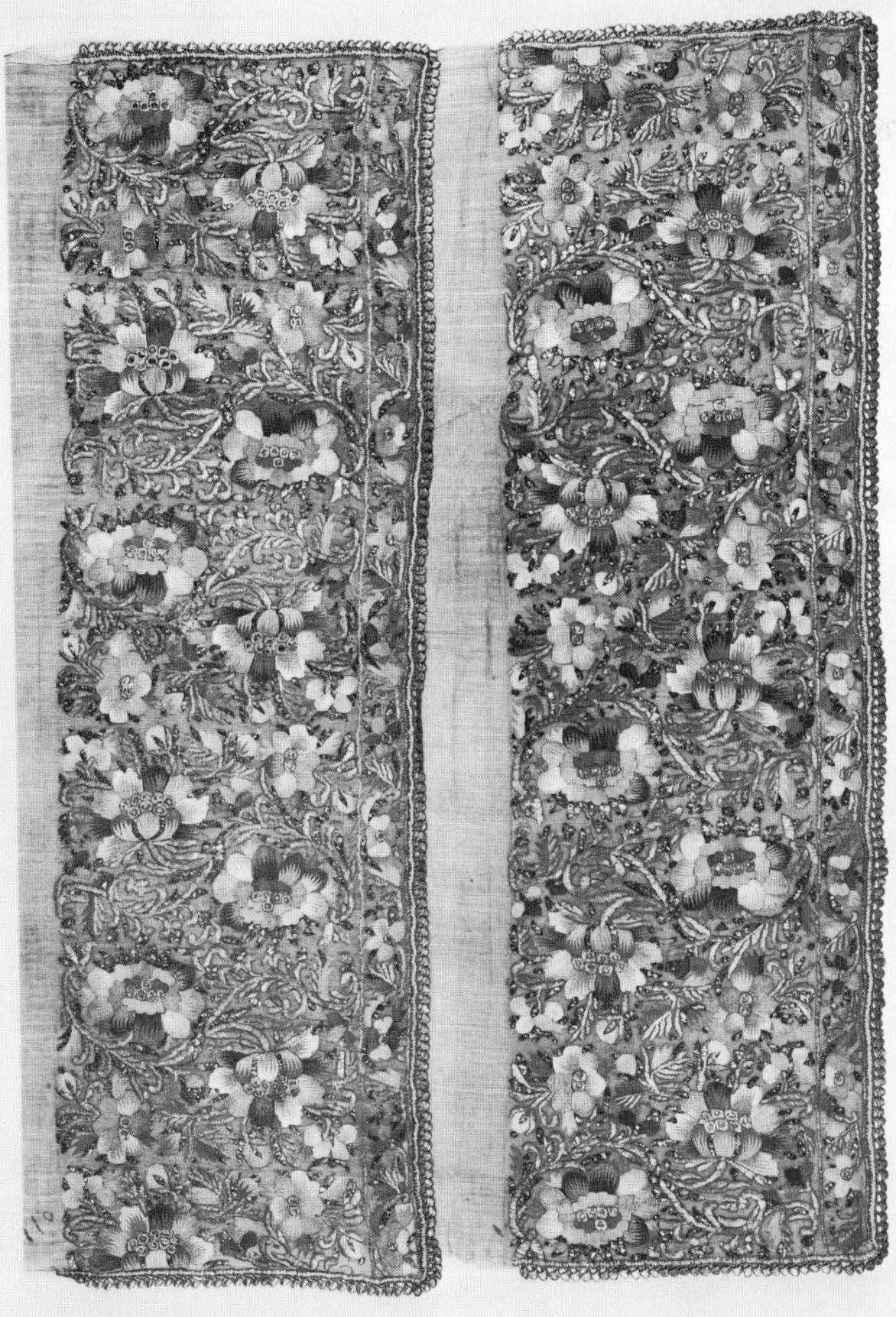

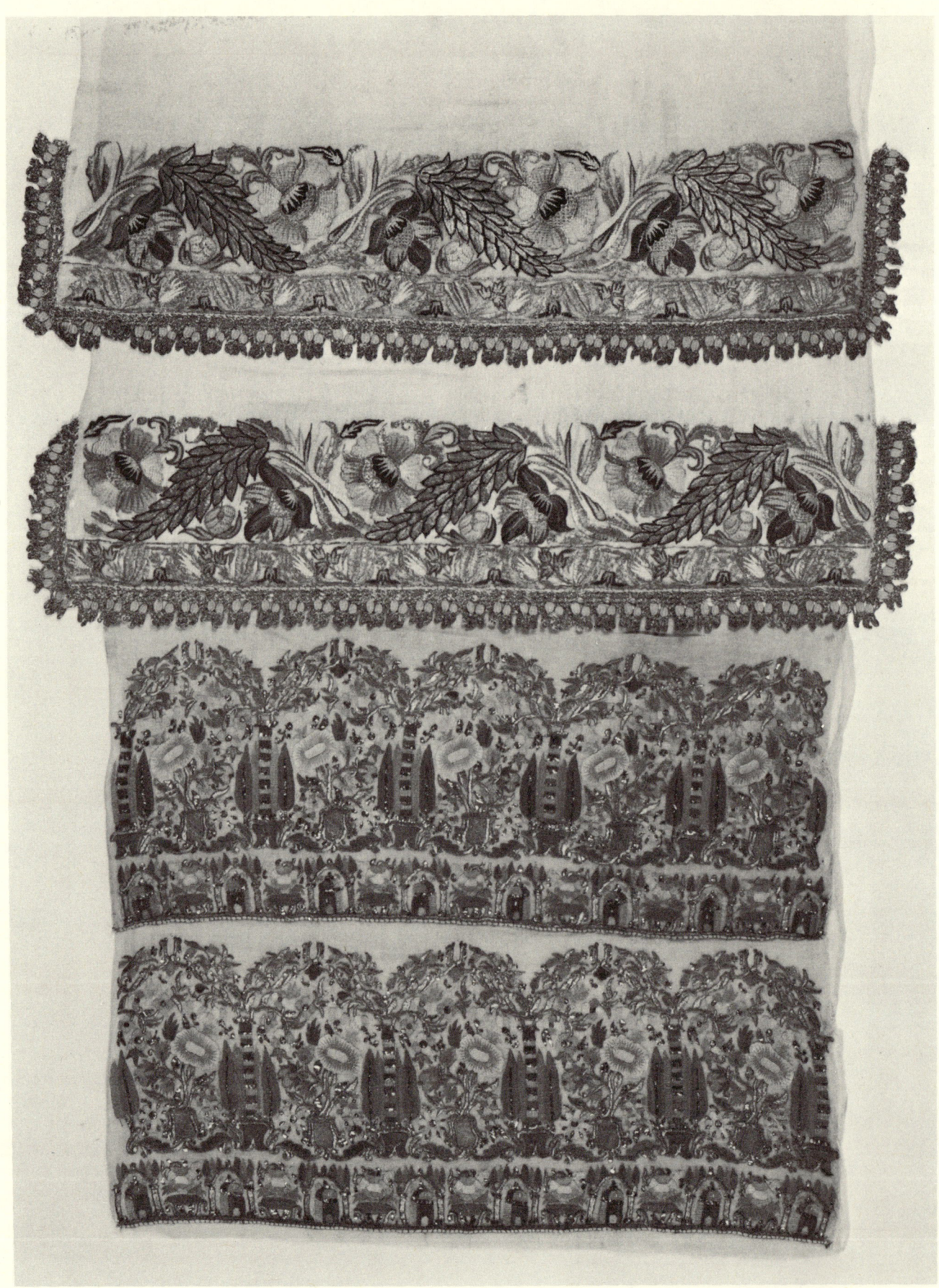

II
The Grand Bazaar

The Grand Bazaar of Istanbul once was the commercial center of the city. Today it remains an important retail center. The first building of the Bazaar, called the Bedestan, or wool market, was built of wood by Sultan Mehmet in 1461. The first expanded Bazaar was built by Sultan Suleiman during his reign (1520-1566). All this was destroyed by a huge conflagration and was reconstructed by succeeding Sultans in stone and brick. This new covered Bazaar was severely damaged by earthquakes in 1844 and 1894 and then rebuilt in the following decades. It is located in the Stambul quarter of Istanbul. It has two

The Nuri Osmaniye entrance to the Grand Bazaar.

main entrances, one opening off the courtyard of the Nuri Osmaniye mosque, and the other near the mosque of Sultan Bayazid II. The courtyard of each mosque is the home of flocks of pigeons, which, as everybody knows, are revered in Moslem lands for the services a pair of their ancestors rendered to Mohammet, the Prophet, at a critical moment in his life. Today some people say that the Bazaar pigeons are harbingers of good for the tourists. It is true that many tourists on passing through a mosque courtyard before entering the Bazaar buy small cups filled with grain which they scatter for the pigeons. Perhaps their actions, like those of their brother tourists who fling coins into the fountain of Trevi in Rome, give them some assurance that their aspirations will be realized.

A broad vaulted avenue connects the two principal entrances of the Bazaar and other wide avenues lead off it and pass around the four sides of the Bedestan, the former wool market, which is today the citadel of the jewelry and antique dealers. In addition to these avenues there is a profusion of narrow streets and lanes covered by vaults and half-domes. There are windows in these through which a dim light filters down giving a touch of magic to many a tawdry object. Each product has its own area, such as furniture, rugs, leather, clothing, shoes, and gold. There are said to be more than three thousand shops in the Bazaar and today there are several restaurants serving the noon meal, a few small religious buildings, a post office, three banks, and a fire and police station. Only pedestrians can enter the portals of the Grand Bazaar, which are closed about seven in the evening and opened about seven each morning except on Sundays and a few Turkish holidays. In the late 1920s old residents said that the Bazaar was losing its Oriental character. This may have seemed true to them, but I found it delightful and very different from any western marketplace that I had seen.

There are eleven lesser doors to the Bazaar, one of which was the principal entrance for tourists when I first saw the Grand Bazaar in 1928. This entrance was at the dead end of Mahmud Pasha Street. Not far before reaching the Bazaar entrance gate on this street was the shop of Sadullah, Levi and Mandil, founded, I was told, in 1868 and housed in 1928 in its own three story Han. On the ground floor in the center of the Han was a fine flagstone courtyard. Originally this was open to the weather but by 1928 a glass skylight at roof level enclosed it. Around the courtyard were offices, receiving areas for carpets, rooms for repairing old carpets, and a cubbyhole for the coffee maker and the carpet spreaders. The walls of the courtyard were decorated with wood screens and carvings that had been a part of the Ottoman pavillion at the World's Fair in Chicago in 1892, and with old Turkish stained glass windows. On the second floor was the great carpet sales room, another room for smaller carpets and rugs, a storeroom for rugs, and a large room for antiquities and Bazaar goods, meaning, at the time, embroideries, brocades, velvets, silver objects, ikons, jewelry, etc., mostly objects from the nineteenth and eighteenth centuries, but sometimes older. A stairway of beautifully carved, painted, and gilded wood gave access to the third floor. On that floor were the workrooms of the carpet designers, looms for weaving—in 1928 the firm had twelve looms constantly working making silk rugs—and a room for the artists who painted and enameled glass mosque lamps. These workrooms were shown to tourists who were usually delighted to see how some of the objects that they purchased in the Bazaar were made.

Mr. Harry Mandil, the managing director, was born in Philadelphia and came to Turkey as a young man. He was very active in American community affairs and was known as "the King of the Bazaars." He was the buying agent in Istanbul for carpets for R. H. Macy & Co. of New York and was respected locally for his knowledge and his integrity. In Istanbul it was said that you did not get bargains at Mandil's but you did get quality, and you could take back a purchase if it didn't look as good at home as it did in the Bazaar, and get your money back. I rarely heard this said of another Bazaar merchant! In 1929 Mr. Mandil's son, Robert, entered the firm and about the same time Mr. Solieman Taney came in as an employee and remained on to become a partner. Getting older and having no children to carry on the business, they decided in 1972 to liquidate the venerable firm. The decision was regretted by a large number of their loyal customers and particularly by me for in more than forty years of association their store had become a regular stop in my Bazaar visits. Beyond Mr. Mandil's on Mahmud Pasha Street, and like him specializing in rugs, brocades, embroideries, old silver, and all manner of decorative objects out of the past, but within the Bazaar gate, was Salih's, then Shalabi's, Moise Asseo's, Elea's, and finally Bitar & Akaoui's. In l928, these were the big names in the Bazaar for "antiquities," although there were many small shops, like those of the four Macedonian brothers in the Bedestan, which made a living from selling such things.

The Macedonians merit special attention. The most active of the four brothers was Turudu Osman Bey. The shop over which he presided was first located in the Bedestan, then in Zingirli Han, and still later again back in the Bedestan. The shop in the Han in the early 1930s was furnished with a low divan for visitors. It occupied one complete side of the room. Around the three other walls were piled huge bales one on top of the other, with some old firearms and sabers stacked in a corner. In these bales were old towels, brocaded dresses and cloaks, military dress uniforms bought to be burned, and the silver metal salvaged from the embroidery, felt prayer rugs, and about every sort of old textile, excepting rugs which Osman did not stock but occasionally handled as a broker. Osman, and to a lesser extent his brothers, knew the stock well and generally made no mistake in selecting at once the bale in which was hidden in some coarser cloth a particularly fine embroidery that he wanted to show to me but this, of course, after offering the traditional cup of Turkish coffee. It is pleasant to observe, as I write this, that Osman's old shop in the Bedestan, now expanded and completely rebuilt, is occupied by his son, Ibrahim. Now there is order and beautiful things on public display, and a modern approach to doing business, but the traditional cup of Turkish coffee remains unchanged.

For archeological objects, there was the shop of Andronikos, a local Greek, in Imaneli Han, just outside one door of the Bazaar, and of Nisan Manoukian, an Armenian, in the Bedestan. During my first years in Istanbul, there were three apprentices at Andronikos': George Zacos, Niko Avgheris, and Petro Hanzaoglou. Each was to carry on an antique business of his own after Andronikos' death until deciding to move elsewhere for personal reasons. At Nisan's, a grandson, Hagop, was an apprentice. He later opened a shop and remained in business, after experiencing some vicissitudes, until he died in 1972, respected and regretted by all who knew him well. Abdullah Kent, a former Imperial Russian cavalry officer, had a rug and furniture shop in Zingirli Han in which he had some archaeological objects. He liked these, and because of this, he sent his son, Mussafer, to the University to study archeology so that later he could continue in business with a wider background than Bazaar experience alone could provide.

In the late 1920s and early 1930s the Bazaar was a social center of Istanbul. In the foreign community it was said that if you wished to meet somebody you had not seen for some time all you had to do was to visit the Bazaar. There was more than an element of truth in this statement as the Bazaar was a magnet that drew everybody. Mrs. Joseph Clark Grew, the wife of the American Ambassador, often accompanied by her daughters Anita and Elsie, or by Betty Carp, was a frequent visitor, as were Mr. Robert Coe, Captain Trammel, and Mr. and Mrs. Julian Gillespie of the Embassy staff. Other prominent Americans often seen there were A. V. Walker, Director of the Socony-Vacuum Oil Company; Thomas Whittemore of the Byzantine Institute; Dean and Mrs. Fisher of Robert College; Mrs. Charles Allen, the wife of the American Consul; Vice Consul and Mrs. Howard Elting, Jr.; Vice Consuls Raymond Hare, Robert English, and William Cramp. Princess Orsini, the wife of the Italian Ambassador, was an almost daily visitor, as was Minister Pozzi of the French Embassy. The British Embassy was represented frequently by Colonel and Mrs. Woods, and the Belgian colony by Mrs. Hanson, the wife of the Director of Electric Power for the city. Baroness de Sorbier de Pougnadoresse, the wife of the Director-General of the Ottoman Bank, was seen quite often in the Bazaar. From the German colony was Mr. Hans von Aulock of the Deutsche Bank, and a whole galaxy of Embassy personnel, Directors of Schools, Professors at the University, etc. The list could grow almost indefinitely but no list would be complete without mentioning Mrs. Lewis Heck, the wife of the General Motors representative, Mrs. Preston King and Mrs. William Johnston, wives of buying agents of American Tobacco Companies, who showed me, each time that I met them some fine trophy that they had just won from the Bazaar.

To appreciate fully the situation it must be remembered that at the time the Bazaar was filled with treasures of the past coming from three sources. First, less than a decade before, the Romanoff dynasty in Russia had been overthrown and the members of the aristocracy had fled the country transporting with them whatever they could salvage from their palaces. Many of these people left Russia by the Black Sea ports and came to Turkey as refugees. Secondly, in Turkey within the decade the dynasty that had ruled the Ottoman Empire for nearly six hundred years had been replaced by a republic, and the scions of the old Imperial family were selling their personal possessions. Thirdly, the reforms of Ataturk, which brought about a wave of modernization and westernization in the living habits of the people prompted the upper and middle classes to use the Bazaar to dispose of many objects which had been a part of the trappings associated with the luxuries of the Oriental life of the past. Perhaps, in addition to the opportunities offered by a rich assortment of merchandise, a reason that made foreigners find the Bazaar an attractive place grew out of the fact that each merchant was waiting in his shop to receive you when you called. He was not conferring with a colleague in Beyoglu, or looking for merchandise in Anatolia, or calling on customers in Europe. Each was at his place in his own shop apparently awaiting your visit, and to the buyer it was indeed pleasant to be welcomed by a familiar smile. Mr. Mandil put it aptly when he said, "In this business you must be lame." And Nisam made the point when he once said to me, "The day before yesterday a man brought me a mortar, and I bought it. Yesterday I was sick at home and the same man brought to my shop a pestle. Today I have a mortar without its pestle."

In 1928 I usually walked from the Consulate to the Bazaar, about a mile and a half, going down Step Street, across Karakoy Square, then the Galata Bridge over the Golden Horn, paying a toll to walk over the bridge, then across Eminonu Square and under the arch over the roadway at Yeni Valide mosque, and through a series of narrow streets to Mahmud Pasha Street, and into the Bazaar. In bad weather I took a tram car on which one safely hopped aboard the open rear platform as the tram slowly rounded a bend in the street before the Consulate building. I got off at Eminonu to walk on to the Bazaar via Mahmud Pasha Street if I was in a hurry, or rode the tram via Sultan Ahmed on to Beyazid Square if time was no object. In 1928 there were few taxis, which nobody thought of using unless he had heavy luggage, some horse carriages, no official or private automobiles at the Consulate, no official and only three private automobiles at the Embassy!

Since it was known generally in the American community that I visited the Bazaar often I was asked by friends to look out for objects that they wanted and which might enter and leave the Bazaar before they realized it. Betty Carp at the Embassy, who was the confidante of everyone, as well as the most kind and helpful person that one could imagine, often asked my help in locating specimens of old Istanbul glass, Beykoz, or Chesme Bulbul, for Mr. Howland Shaw, who fancied them but was unable to give much time to searching as he was nearly always on duty in Ankara as the Counsellor of the Embassy delegation there. I knew very little about old glass but I sometimes took a likely piece on consignment for Betty to send to Mr. Shaw, wrapping it always in the story of its discovery. Sometimes, according to Betty, Mr. Shaw liked the story as much as the glass and so I was encouraged to include all the local flavor. That was easy for me, but I did worry about the authenticity of some of the glasses that the stories sold! This later proved unnecessary as Mr. Shaw, on leaving Turkey, presented his collection of glass to the Seraglio Museum in Istanbul. The authorities pronounced it all genuine, displayed it handsomely in a special case in a fine location where it remains until this day.

In the winter of 1931 I wrote to Mr. Shaw: "I went out to your house with Miss Carp this afternoon in order to see your Beykoz things. They are very pretty in a quaint, old fashioned way. But how do you know that they are Beykoz? I am anxious to learn about glass as it is a subject of which I am completely ignorant. I spent two holidays searching in the library of Robert College but I didn't find a word written on Beykoz glass! In the Chinili Kiosk there is a case of beautiful glass labelled "Beykoz," and the man who collected these pieces gave me a lecture on the characteristics of the glass. I checked his facts with Heim (an antiquities merchant in Beyoglu) and learned that the former gentleman is completely wrong, according to Heim. I am sure that I would be in an awful muddle over the question if it were not for the advice of one of the four Macedonian brothers who said: 'Keep to towels, Mr. Berry. It is safer. Seventy percent of the glass that is sold in Istanbul as Beykoz is made in Venice, twenty percent of it is made in Bohemia, ten percent at the Yildiz Kiosk, and only five percent at Beykoz!' "

The following is an extract from a letter written to Mr. Shaw on May 27, 1931, which accompanied a piece of old Turkish glass sent to him on approval:

"The American: 'But what is it? A miniature gin bottle?'
"The Englishman: 'It looks to me like a little vinegar cruet. Doesn't it to you?'

"The Turk: 'My dear fellows, you are asking questions to which there are no answers. Nobody knows what this little piece of Chesme Bulbul glass was intended for except the man who ordered it, and he has been dead at least one hundred years. *You* may name it a vinegar cruet and you may be right. At least I will not be the one to say that you are wrong. But for me it is a surahi, and probably one made to hold Zemzem water for the day when it would be needed.

"'You know that every pious Moslem makes a pilgrimage to Mecca at least once in his lifetime. He visits the holy places of that city and, of course, among them the well of Zemzem. As the well contains holy water it was and is much revered by the faithful. Little tins of it are brought back home by the Hadjis, much as some Christians bring back water from the River Jordan for christenings, except that we administer Zemzem water to the dying rather than to the newly born.

"'It is probable that someone had made this little carafe to preserve some water brought from the well of Zemzem at Mecca. Its size and its beauty indicate that it was used to contain some precious liquid. To a Moslem it is logical to conclude that that precious liquid was Zemzem water. But,' and he said this with a twinkle in his eye, 'I can also understand how an Englishman would think that it was made for vinegar, and an American for gin.'"

Chesme Bulbul Surabi. Nineteenth century. Turkish.

Although the archaeologists tended to disparage Chesme Bulbul glass, there was plenty of other glass and pottery in the Bazaar to interest them. Most of the archaeological glass was of the Roman period and came to the Bazaar from all parts of Turkey. It was usually in the form of clear or green-tinted, free-blown bottles and jugs made for holding liquids. Smaller pieces, made for cosmetics, were of amber or blue glass and were often ornamented with trailings in other colors. Still more beautiful were the opaque glass vessels blown around a sand core and known in the Bazaar as "Phoenician." Besides the glass there was usually a considerable quantity of old pottery available. It was principally Roman, but, after the excavation of some Yortan sites, large quantities of Yortan ware became available. Later, when the Hacilar digs were opened, some Hacilar ware was found in the Bazaar. At the time original Roman terracotta lamps sold two for a dollar and the Yortan vessels were just as inexpensive. Those prices made it uneconomic to imitate them, but the Hacilar figurines caught the public fancy and were imitated and sold at good prices almost as soon as the first original pieces reached the Istanbul Bazaar.

Amphoiskos of ivory and brown glass. Sixth to fourth century B.C. *called Phoenician.*

In addition to letters about Bazaar objects, Mr. Shaw urged me to write to him about the Bazaar people. Included here are sections from two such letters. They may contribute to the understanding of the Grand Bazaar as it was in 1928.

"A lady once asked me: 'How can you find the Grand Bazaar interesting? It is *so* dirty.' And then in the same breath she complained of her husband's ill luck in being sent to a city where there was so little to divert one. In Istanbul there is no music, no theatre, nothing to entertain a person, so she said.

"But I ask, where could one find a more entertaining theatre than the Bazaar? I think that it is by all odds the most amazing and delightful theatre that I have ever attended. In it there are a thousand stages where act a thousand casts in which each actor plays his part well. Elea, Turudu Osman, and Merinsky are among the Bazaar's greatest actors. Their shops, that is to say the stages on which they put on their performances, are, as the lady said, more or less dirty. But these Bazaar stages are only physically dirty.

"In looking for some embroideries this afternoon I stopped in to see Elea, who, besides being an actor, is also an aristocrat among the Bazaar merchants. In his shop I uncovered a towel that pleased me and, when I offered a smaller sum for it than the one that he first suggested he said, very haughtily, that he would prefer to see his merchandise rotting on the shelves and his children dying of starvation than to besmirch the name of Elea by bargaining over the price of a towel! Appearing to be impressed by his sincerity I rose and as I walked toward the door remarked that I should never ask the House of Elea to deviate from its traditional policy, nor should I deviate from my policy of never buying without bargaining! Elea, the actor, with even a grander manner than he had first used, repeated, 'The House of Elea never bargains,' then, smiling benevolently he added, 'but, on occasion, it does graciously reduce its prices to meet the size of the purse of its customers that it desires to please!'

"What an actor that fellow is! He steps out of one role and into another with perfect ease, and, best of all, without breaking the spell that he has over his audience. That is acting the like of which one looks for but does not always see on the professional stage.

Grape cluster flask of purple blown glass. Second century A.D., Roman.

"And with what care the stage is set! There is always a profusion of objects, some new things placed with the old in such a way that the contrast makes old rubbish appear to be fine antiques. This impression of age is enhanced by the dim light that filters through the dust-laden atmosphere from the small windows, semi-opaque with grime, in the domes of the roof. With the streets around these shops crowded by a motley throng of individuals who shout to one another in any one of half a dozen languages what an atmosphere is created! Of course it is irresistible to groups of tourists fresh from the sales counters of American stores. And when these tourists arrive what stories are told them in the name of truth and what trifles are exchanged for gold!

"The professors explain this phenomenon by attributing it to a thing called Bazaar fever, but to most of us it is nothing more than good play acting. It is accomplished because a capable actor is playing upon a scene where the stage mechanics are properly adjusted to assist him in his part. I cannot see how anyone who really cares for the theatre could be disappointed in the Bazaar. It is a school of competitive acting. It is an example of the Little Theatre grown up.

"The Bazaar, when you look at it as a theatre, has another unique feature. It is the only theatre that I have ever attended where you pay, if satisfied, at the end of the performance and then, after paying for the show, receive a present. The present is not often very valuable but the memory of the story that goes with it is usually well worth the cost. But one must never doubt the story, for to doubt it breaks the spell and ruins its value forever.

"Young Merinsky helped me to understand this point. I complained to him that a dish he had sold to me did not fit into the story that he gave me with the dish. In the story the dish was solid silver while the one that I bought, I discovered when I got home, was plated ware. But that, it appeared, was my fault for, he said, 'If I had told you that the dish was metal plated with silver you would have been disappointed, and I could not bring myself to disappoint you!' "

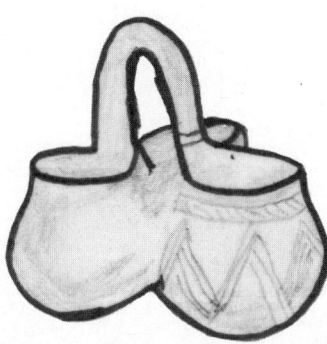

Early Bronze Age pottery from a Yortan grave. Three pots forming a single vessel. Earthenware. The design is incised.

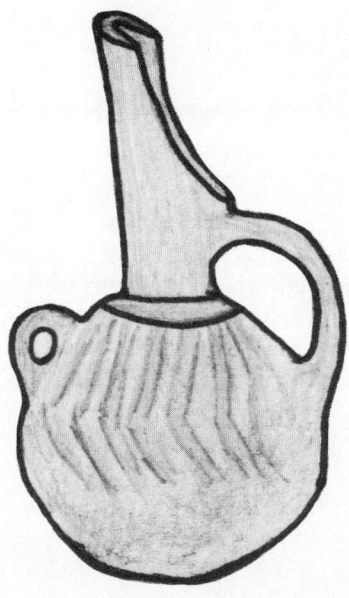

Early Bronze Age pottery from a Yortan grave. A pitcher. Earthenware. Decoration in relief.

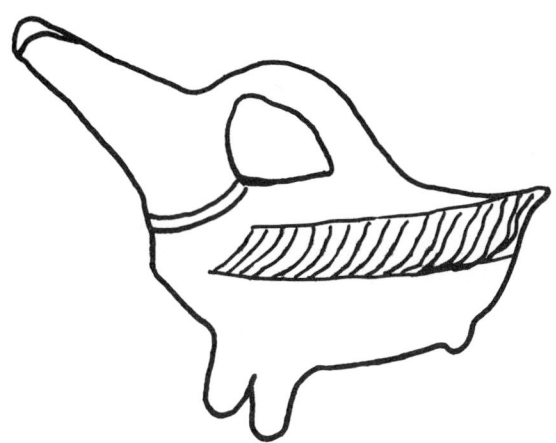

Early Bronze Age pottery from a Yortan grave. A pitcher in the form of a fowl. Earthenware. The design is incised.

One bleak winter weekend I went to the Bazaar on Friday afternoon and encountered a blanket of depression as thick as a proverbial London fog. I wrote Mr. Shaw of it saying that most exceptionally there was nothing newly purchased in the market to study, there were no new stories about tourists, there was little movement of people in the Bazaar streets, and nobody in the shops but dull and bored shopkeepers. As the Bazaar is seldom this way I started to talk to the shopkeepers, asking them about the "good old days" and particularly about the work that each had done before he became an "antikaji." Mr. Mandil, I learned, had sold hats in New York and his partner, Talat Bey, worked beside his father making and selling combs. Mr. Heim, whom I met in the street an hour later, said that he had made a fortune in the paper business before he set up shop as an antiquarian. The man that we call Bitar, whose real name is Michel Akaoui, was upon the point of becoming a priest when fate, acting through the death of a relative who was a Bazaar merchant, put him in charge of a Bazaar shop with the added responsibility of educating several nephews. The afternoon passed quickly for me and with each visit I received a new surprise. Elea, I discovered, was once a cobbler and Riza explained—rather proudly, I thought—that he had lived by being a sort of super-gigolo until he "grew tired." Apparently his early training was helpful as he is now highly successful in selling to the ladies.

With my call on Riza, the "blue mood" long left behind, I stopped plying questions and, as it was growing late, went home to dinner.

Saturday I again returned to the Bazaar. I had found my Friday afternoon talks amusing, and continued my inquiries among the silversmiths. Ivanoff said that he was a jeweler in Russia and Abdullah was a cavalry officer in the Caucasus. Halit, until the death of his father who had a shelf in the Bedestan, gained his livelihood by raising and lowering the curtains on the stage of a theatre in Beyoglou. The boy known as "Halit's brother," and who was really the son of Halit's second wife's first husband, dug drains until his stepmother made a fortunate marriage. Vartan said that his former profession was being classically educated for many years through the charity of a wealthy American lady but the depression in America cut short that life and as a result he was now happily engaged in making silver filagree. I finished the day with a call on the young Merinsky. This gentleman informed me that he once was a counterfeiter in Russia but he gave up that profession because he heard that it was easier to make money selling antiques in Istanbul. In Russia, he said, his faked rubles had to *look* like the real thing, while in Istanbul all that he needed to do in order to sell new silver for old was to *tell* the customer that it was old. A customer, entering the shop then interrupted our conversation and I left immediately rather than witness a demonstration of his salesmanship.

How can one feel "blue" for long with such people about?

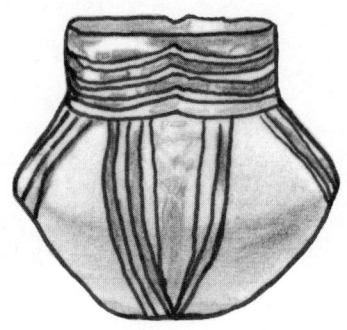

Earthenware jar from Hacilar, c. 5000 B.C.

And after I was transferred from Istanbul and Mr. Shaw had left Ankara for Washington he would occasionally write to me about some promising young officer who was being assigned to Istanbul. He would suggest that, if I knew the young man, I write to him as my enthusiasm for the Bazaar and Turkey might prove contagious. One such letter to a friend and successor in the Consulate General at Istanbul follows:

"So Bursa captivated you too! I thought that it would, and I believe that the more you see of that charming old city the more you will come to love her. At least that was my experience. The next time you make the trip, have a look around for Halici Yusuf Effendi. He is a very old man who in fine weather sits in front of his door in one of the old hans near the Bazaar. I can't give you precise directions for locating the han but it is one of those massive Turkish brick structures built around a great courtyard. Along the four sides of the court there is a wide porch which serves as a corridor for the tenants of the han. Yusuf Effendi's door is on the upper floor in the far corner to the left of the stairs and if he is still living he will be seated in front of his door. You will recognize him at once by his well-kept white beard or ask Betty Carp for his photo—I gave one to her.

"It was on my second trip to Bursa that I heard that one Yusuf Effendi had some finely embroidered towels. I sought him out to see his towels. He did have some nice pieces but he esteemed them too highly for me to hope to buy and so over our coffee we talked about old towels much more philosophically than one does when a bargain is about to be reached. It was such a pleasant experience that on each subsequent visit to Bursa I called at Yusuf Effendi's door and we talked about towels and other things. On one of these visits I said to him, 'Since these towels of yours have such great value why not go to Istanbul and sell them? You can place the money in a bank for use as you need it. Then you won't have to sit by your door late into the evening waiting for the buyer who doesn't come!'

" 'What you have said, my friend, others have said, and it is all true. But let us suppose that last year I had sold my towels and placed 5000 liras in a bank in Istanbul. Would you have searched out this old man?' And after a pause he added, 'Someday you too will understand, Mr. Berry, that coffee drunk alone is not sweet.'

"Yes, I think that you too will like Yusuf Effendi."

A letter to Elbert Mathews, an esteemed colleague of my last tour of duty in the State Department and later a successor as American Consul General at Istanbul, must close this chapter. It was written from Baghdad in late September, 1952.

"This is the time of year when one of the things I liked most to do in Istanbul was to drive out through the Adrianople gate about six in the morning to about a mile beyond the great barracks, then turn to the right passing them and starting down the hill above Eyub. I would stop half way down the hill, sit in the early morning sunshine and watch the mist above the Golden Horn dissipate and the city, with its domes and minarets, gradually come into view. Then, on those Sundays or holidays at this time of year when I felt a touch of nostalgia, I would go out to Beykoz and walk through the fallen leaves in the park of the old casino. They rustle exactly like real Indiana leaves. At this time of year, too, I liked to resume my late afternoon Bazaar visits sometimes sitting and talking for an hour with one of the shopkeepers with his merchandise spread around him, but with no strong impulse for me to buy or for him to sell. I came to appreciate that some of these men, who at first acquaintance appeared to be unmitigated scoundrels, were really very fine people having strong impulses of generosity, humanitarianism, and tolerance. All such experiences contributed toward my education, pleasure in living, and spiritual well-being with the result that I think of Istanbul with gratitude and affection. I hope that your own experience will give you the same satisfaction both now and in the future."

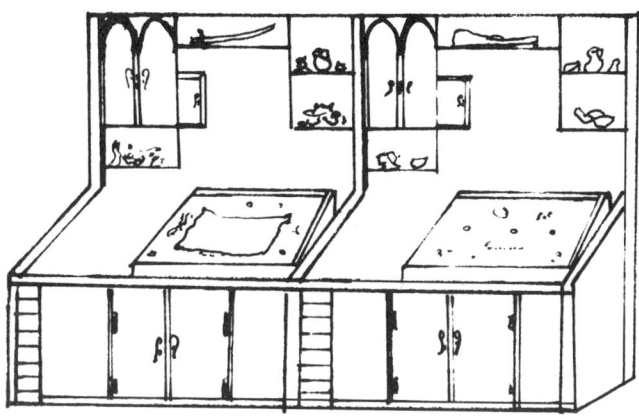

A "shelf" or shop in the Bedestan, typical of all Bedestan shops in 1928. A single example survived until 1974.

The Grand Bazaar

Plates for Chapter II

		Page
19.	A map of the Grand Bazaar of Istanbul as drawn in 1931 by William M. Cramp.	61
20.	The courtyard of the Nuri Osmaniye mosque. (BYB-1973.)	62
21.	The Mahmud Pasha Street entrance to the Bazaar. (BYB-1972.)	63
22.	The principal western entrance to the Bazaar near the mosque of Sultan Bayazid II. (BYB-1972.)	64
23.	The courtyard of Zingirli Han contains several shops where antiques are sold and, on the second floor, the workrooms of a rug repairer. (BYB-1972.)	65
24.	The stall of a brass and copper merchant in the Bedestan. (BYB-1972.)	66
25.	The afternoon sun pierces the Bazaar shadows with shafts of light. (BYB-1942.)	67
26.	The principal East-West street of the Bazaar seen from near the Nuri Osmaniye mosque entrance. (BYB-1973.)	68
27.	In Zingirli Han the owner of a shop selling archaeological objects and his customer. (BYB-1942.)	69

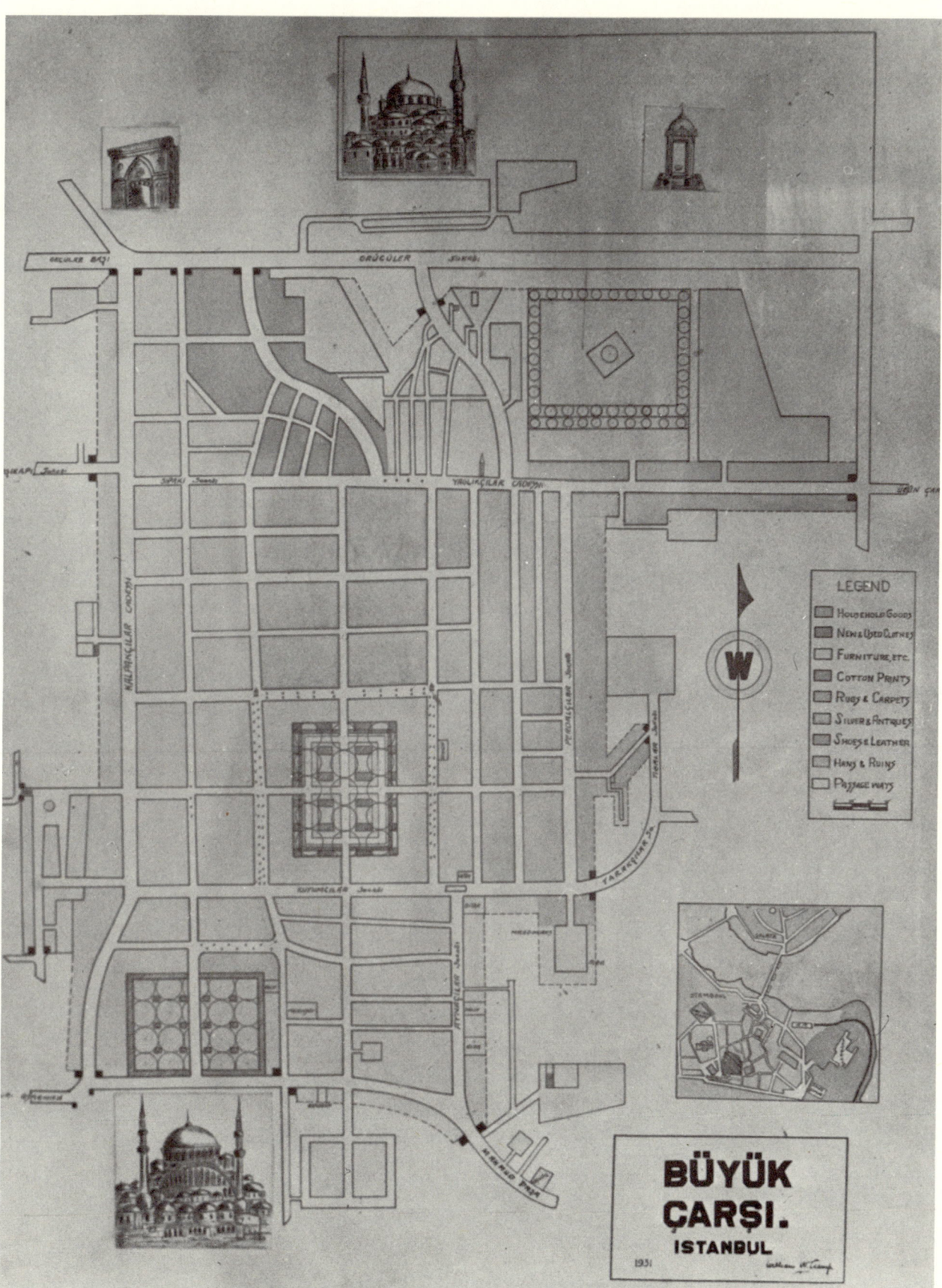

III

Rugs, Carpets, Brocades, and Velvets

When it came to rugs and carpets Mr. Mandil was my mentor. They were his life and because of this he was an expert salesman. He liked to share his knowledge and his enthusiasm and over the years I benefited greatly from both. Most of Mr. Mandil's business was in modern rugs but his real interest was in the antiques and semi-antiques. Some modern rugs came from Anatolia but most of the rugs that went to America were made in Persia, shipped to the Customs Transit warehouse in Istanbul, viewed there by prospective buyers, and then shipped to their ultimate destination without the payment of a customs duty in Turkey. The antique and semi-antique rugs were brought to the market by brokers who carried them over their shoulders from shop to shop until a buyer was found.

Definitions vary in different places and at different times, but when I went to Istanbul a modern rug was defined as one freshly cut from the loom; that is, unused. A semi-antique rug was one made sometime in the recent past, perhaps forty or fifty or more years ago, and showing usage. An antique rug was one made at least one hundred years ago, usually in the nineteenth or eighteenth centuries, but occasionally even in the seventeenth century. It was much used and often threadbare. I never saw or heard of a carpet or rug made before 1600 as having been sold in the Istanbul Bazaar. It must be remembered that a rug used in Turkey in a home or mosque for, say forty years, would show much less wear than a similar rug used for a like period of time in an American or European home or public building. The reason is that in both homes and mosques in Turkey people walked around in slippers or in stocking feet.

In going to and coming from the Bazaar on my daily trip I always stopped to greet Mr. Mandil and exchange a pleasantry over a cup of coffee. He would show what he had purchased that day, or what had come back from the repair weavers. Any used carpet that he bought had to be put into shape before he placed it in his stock for sale.

Repairing was often a long and tedious process. It developed like this: A broker arriving from Anatolia would bring his stock to the courtyard of Mr. Mandil's han. Each bale would be opened and the pieces shown one by one. Mr. Mandil would eliminate what did not interest him and, when the whole lot had been inspected, return to the selected pieces to bargain over the price. This was sometimes a long drawn-out performance, occasionally charged with emotion and drama, interspersed with curses and threats by the broker to carry away his disputed merchandise and never again darken the door of the firm. Sometimes a deal was consummated and sometimes not. Once in a while a purchase was made as easily as buying a newspaper from a newsstand. When an antique rug was purchased it looked to a newcomer, as I was in 1928, like something to be thrown away, as indeed the former owner usually thought. It was often stained, the ends ravelled, holes and tears in the center, threadbare in places, and so out of shape that it would not lie flat on the floor. The first step in restoration was to brush the rug thoroughly with side motions of a broom made of twigs, and then to decide whether to risk washing it. This was always a serious decision for a color might run in washing or develop different and unpleasant tones. Also, if the pile was worn down to the knots, the rug might even disintegrate in the washing. The problem was to keep the patina of age while reviving the original beauty of the colors. After washing, and sometimes before, the master repair weaver was called in. He made his estimate of the time and cost to put the rug back into usable shape. If his estimate was acceptable, he took the rug away with him to his workroom. There each area of the rug that required attention was in turn nailed to a small loom, which an apprentice weaver, seated on the floor, held on her knees while she refilled the holes and torn places and reinforced the badly worn areas with new wool. When all of the repairs were completed, the pile was cut down to a uniform height and the rug was nailed pile downward on the wooden floor. Every morning it was sprinkled with water which in drying shrunk the rug into the shape that it was meant to have. When the weaver was satisfied that his work was done he removed the nails. In place of the rag that he had carried away he would bring back to Mr. Mandil a beautiful old textile that not only appeared to be in perfect condition but would lay flat on the floor! This work often required months of skilled labor and sometimes cost several times the original purchase price of the rug.

My first sojourn in Turkey occurred during the period when Ataturk was launching his far-reaching reform movements. As a result of these, modernization was the order of the day in both the public and private sectors of the community. These reforms had a direct bearing on the quantity of "antiques" coming into the Bazaar. Mr. Mandil told me that whereas for years before the reforms he had seen three or four antique carpets a month suddenly they began to arrive by the bale! Where did they all come from? Some came from private houses whose owners, in the spirit of the time, wished to modernize their furnishings. But the greater number of the rugs came out of the mosques and tekkes throughout the country. Most of these rugs were commonplace, had long ago outlived their usefulness, and should have been replaced years ago. But some among them were really excellent old pieces. Generally, these came from the mihrabs of the mosques, which in Islamic countries are normally adorned by a particularly fine prayer rug. The choice rugs reaching the Bazaar from these sources were for the most part seventeenth and eighteenth century prayer rugs made at Kula, Ghordes, or Bergama in Asia Minor. Each of these rugs needed to be passed through the hands of the repair weaver to be put into shape for the Western buyer. But even before restoration they were truly beautiful textiles which bore eloquent testimony to the skill of the Turkish weavers of by-gone times.

I recall visiting Mr. Mandil's shop one day in 1929. I found him in a jubilant mood for he had just purchased five magnificent, large antique carpets. "Not one, but five," he repeated. There were one Ispahan, two Ardibils, and two dragon Kubas. Hadib Edib Bey, the Turkish connoisseur, took the Ispahan and one Ardibil for his Swiss chateau where they were greatly admired by all who saw them. Baron Henri de Rothschild took the second Ardibil, telling Mr. Mandil that for fifteen years he had been searching for a carpet of that age, size, and quality for the drawing room of his Paris house. The larger Kuba was bought for the new residence of Prince Paul, then the Regent of Yugoslavia. The smaller Kuba eventually found its ultimate home at Colonial Williamsburg, Virginia. At the time, the story was told that these rugs were bought from a broker who had purchased them from a mosque in a town near the Iraqi frontier—which side of the frontier was never made completely clear. According to the story, the broker, acting the part of the pious Moslem, had offered, in the spirit of the time, to recarpet the mosque floor with modern thick-pile carpets in exchange for the threadbare ones then on the floor. After due deliberation the offer was accepted. The new carpets arrived and were put into place to the rejoicing of the community, the donor's name was inscribed on a roll of honor, and he departed for Istanbul to sell his coup to Mr. Mandil at a pretty profit. The five carpets took more than two years to come out of the repair weavers' room but when they did they were real beauties. It seemed at the time that every foreign local resident and many tourists wanted to buy one or more antique rugs for his home but there were really no local collectors, properly speaking. The greatest Oriental rug collection made in my lifetime, that I was aware of, was assembled by Mr. Joseph V. McMullan. Although he found his treasures in New York rather than in the Istanbul Bazaar, some of his prizes had reached New York via Istanbul.

When buying antique Kula and Ghordes rugs Mr. Mandil always hoped to come across a Transylvania rug. A Transylvania rug is really nothing more than a copy of a Kula or Ghordes made in the seventeenth or eighteenth century in Transylvania. They came about in this way. The rich merchants of Brasov and other cities of Transylvania journeyed to Istanbul annually to sell and buy goods. When they did well on their trips each brought back home as a present for his wife a Kula or Ghordes carpet. The lady habitually placed this carpet on the seat of the family pew in the local church where it advertised her husband's success in business and made the cold hard pew more comfortable for the family during church services. Some churches in Transylvania, the Black church at Brasov particularly, have, even today, a large collection of these carpets, which, now suspended from the balcony, add a soft colorful note to the austere beauty of the building. Of course, in the congregation there were merchants who had not made the trip to Istanbul, or were not too successful in their business, and the wives of many of these men urged them to do their duty by their family and church. It was a case of keeping up with the Joneses, and so carpets were made in Transylvania which imitated the Kulas and Ghordes. These were lovely carpets and in time a group of amateurs developed who cherished them above all other antique carpets—and paid accordingly!

Mr. Mandil liked to talk about his customers and of their purchases and sometimes he was the butt of his own stories, and this added to his stature in my eyes. Once he told me of a Mrs. Vanderbilt who bought from him a pair of magnificent Caucasian antique kilims for use as portieres between two drawing rooms in her New York house. They created a sensation and as a result one of her would-be rivals in the New York social world came to Istanbul in 1920 and sought out Mr. Mandil. She told him that she absolutely had to have a similar pair of kilims, but of course superior and that money was no objective. Mr. Mandil was indefatigable in his efforts to please the lady, and some years later his industry was rewarded and a magnificent pair of Caucasian kilims surfaced. They were even finer than Mrs. Vanderbilt's. But by this time the New York lady was dead and the style in portieres had changed! Mr. Mandil ruefully added, "I should have gone into the woman's wear business where you know that styles change every season!"

Styles in what was "right" in Oriental carpets did change often. For a time Mr. Mandil could not find enough semi-antique Caucasians to supply the demand. Then suddenly there was no demand for Caucasians, but people were asking for Anatolians, Melas, and Bergamas, particularly. Silk rugs were very popular in some circles in the 1920s but the stock market crash and following depression ended their boom. When the boom ended many Oriental merchants who had silk carpets on their looms were forced to complete the weaving, often at the cost of many months of labor, only to have a stock of unsalable products! As styles in material, wool, and silk shifted, and styles in period and places of origin, so did style in size. Once it was de rigueur in a fashionable household to have a single large rug covering the floor of a room with only a narrow border of parquet showing around it. Then somebody invented machine-made wall-to-wall carpeting and the demand for the large hand-made Oriental carpets decreased rapidly. Small, brightly colored antique scatter rugs were sometimes used on the modern wall-to-wall carpets, but these wall-to-wall machine-made carpets, plus the emergence of inexpensive hand-made attractive large carpets from China, caused the great boom in Oriental carpets to end with the 1920s.

Once in talking with Mr. Mandil about a rug merchant's problem of what to stock and a collector's problem of what and when to buy, he summarized his thinking for me: "Successful merchants and successful collectors should anticipate the trend. They should buy what is available, but not available everywhere in quantity, because for the collector the lure is in discovery. When the supply is extremely limited or exhausted the collectors quickly lose interest. In such circumstances even the dedicated collector, when he can be ferreted out by the merchant, usually already has in his collection the 'unique' piece that is now offered to him. In short, the most successful merchant or collector must ride the wave just before the crest breaks."

Mr. Mandil did not bargain over prices in his shop, but in the winter of 1928-9 he occasionally sold me some minor object from his stock leaving it at a price well under the marked selling price. As I chose the best of what was available I felt some twinges of conscience, and I told my supervising officer at the Consulate, Consul Charles Allen, of my feelings. He reassured me saying that antiquities to Mr. Mandil were like potatoes to a grocer. Some of the grocer's customers fancied small potatoes and some large, but the grocer was only interested in selling potatoes. This little lesson served me well throughout my Bazaar life and rarely thereafter was I, the buyer, to assume a feeling of responsibility for the actions of the seller.

Rugs, Carpets, Brocades, and Velvets

But now, in re-reading this, I find it necessary to qualify the statement a bit. One's objective, of course, was to acquire what was wanted at an acceptable price. But at the same time it was necessary to always leave the seller satisfied with the price that he had agreed to. The seller must not feel that he has been taken in by a more informed person. A sale often turned on this latter point and in resolving it much Oriental savoir faire was brought into play. I recall one day I sat watching Mr. Mandil bargain for an antique Kula prayer rug. The price was finally agreed to, the deal apparently finished, when the seller suddenly picked up the rug, threw it across his shoulders, and started to go away murmuring that perhaps he was being taken as a fool! Mr. Mandil smiled and pointed to a small blue bead tied to the fringe of the rug. It was enough. The seller *knew* that the blue bead would assure protection from the evil eye, in this case the rapaciousness of a Bazaar rug merchant, and so the deal was completed with assurance.

Perhaps here I shall have to borrow the flying carpet of Ali Baba to effect the transition from carpet buying in the Bazaars of Istanbul in 1928 to a scene at the local American Embassy and another on the Bosphorus, both of which supplement the blue bead episode observed at Mr. Mandil's, to show how essential it was for living happily in a Near Eastern community to appreciate the other person's thought processes.

At the time this occurred I was a Third Secretary at the Embassy, the most junior position in the diplomatic hierarchy. I had among my duties the responsibility of the maintenance of the garden plot in the Embassy compound in Istanbul. The secretary on duty was required to keep a diary for the information of both the Ambassador (when he was away from the city) and the delegation at Ankara. As very little that was important occurred when the high officials were away, we secretaries had to make copy by recording trivia. The story that follows I have taken from a page of my diary to Ambassador Skinner.

"A few weeks ago I wrote to the man in London who purchases for me in England the things that I need. I told him that I had been put in charge of a small garden plot, that I knew nothing at all about gardening, and that, in spite of this handicap, I wished to do well the task to which I was assigned. I asked him to search the bookstores of London in order to find for me a proper book on gardening. I specified that it must be scientific, and yet practical, comprehensive, but brief; scholarly, and at the same time simple. In a word, the only book which I wanted was the one book that precisely fitted my needs. In due time a package came from London by book post, and on opening it I found a small volume entitled *Gardening for the Ignorant*.

"On first reading I found this volume a bit too advanced for me. However, after several visits to the gardens of a local florist, a call at the municipal plant nursery, and the help of many local friends who have gardens, I mastered its contents. In fact I have progressed to the point where I understand something of soil chemistry and plant breeding. I even have now *The Blue Book of Gardening* upon my desk, and quote from it upon occasion.

"This morning, as there was a warm south wind blowing and a feel of spring in the air, I decided that it was time to put to practical use the knowledge that I had amassed. I went to the garden and with the aid of an interpreter I 'helped' the gardener with my scientific advice for two hours. Being rather tired at the end of that time I returned to my office in order to observe from the window what success my efforts produced. I had no more than reached my window when I saw the gardener take a blue bead from his pocket, hang the bead on the garden gate, and then 'knock off' work for the remainder of the day. Superstitious local people believe, of course, that a blue bead placed on a door will provide protection from the evil eye!"

During the early years of the financial depression there were no promotions, our allowances were cut, and money was generally short. I continued to visit the Bazaar, but as I could buy little I went less often and developed as a substitute for my Bazaar visits a project to photograph all the antique public fountains along the Bosphorus many of which were threatened by the modernization program. I often wrote Mr. Shaw of my excursions. Here is an extract from one such letter:

"I went over to Scutari Sunday to take some photographs, and, as Ali Nadji Bey, the kindly and knowledgeable dragoman at the Consulate, lives over there, I asked him to walk about with me. We looked at fountains, and tiles, and whatnots without end, and, just for the sake of changing the subject, I said that I should like to photograph a particularly fine cypress tree that was growing in the garden of the mosque where we happened to be at the moment.

" 'It will make a better picture if you photograph the tree from the mosque porch,' Ali Bey suggested.

" 'Good,' I replied. 'We'll take it from the porch.'

" 'But it will be best to ask permission first.'

" 'Alright, ask permission.'

" 'And it would be courteous to offer the guardian of the mosque a small present, say three or four Turkish pounds.'

" 'THREE OR FOUR TURKISH POUNDS! Why, Ali Bey, that is more money than that old fellow makes in a week!'

" 'That is true, Mr. Berry, but you must pay it. The guardian thinks that you have come over to Scutari and walked up a long hill just to photograph that tree. To go to so much trouble in order to get a photograph means that the photograph must be valuable. So, as you are going to profit much from the picture of the tree, it is only fair that its guardian share a little in your gain.' "

When I was in Istanbul first it was fashionable for the ladies in the foreign communities of the city to cover the coffee tables in their living rooms and sofa cushions with lovely old Turkish and Persian brocaded silks. This material came from nineteenth and eighteenth and sometimes seventeenth century cloaks. These were in silks of all colors ornamented with woven floral or geometric designs in silver, or silver-gilt thread. Like the embroideries the cloaks were brought to the Bazaar in great bales by peddlers who tramped Anatolia to buy old clothes. The cloaks were sold to antique dealers, paid for according to

Ogival design on a seventeenth-century Turkish brocade.

Rugs, Carpets, Brocades, and Velvets

their beauty and condition, and then carefully ripped apart at the seams. The back of each cloak usually furnished one panel of loom-width material large enough to make a cover for a coffee table. Then the pieces from the other parts of the cloak were assembled into two or three squares to be used for making cushion covers. This required patience and skill as the tiny fragments had to be joined so that the finished pillow covers appeared to be made from a single piece of material. Sometimes scraps that could not be used in making cushion covers were used to make a lady's evening handbag. These old brocades were really beautiful and when remade into pillow or table covers they gave a plain room a touch of luxury. They were very popular as long as the supply of cloaks continued to come to the market, but after a few years the sources of the supply became exhausted, and so the style of interior decoration had to change and something beautiful was lost. Nowadays one rarely sees an old brocade in the Bazaar and when a piece does turn up it remains unsold because nobody knows what to do with it!

The velvets available were older than the brocades, some dating from the sixteenth century. They were originally woven for covers of the hard pillows of Turkish divans, for hangings, and to be made into clothing. They were much rarer and more expensive to buy than the brocades and, because of their stiffness, were more difficult to use in a modern house. However, a double panel of dark red velvet with a rich ogival or floral design woven in silver-gilt thread made a very handsome wall hanging for any great room in an Embassy or private mansion. These double panels were exceedingly rare even in my early Bazaar life. Today I recall seeing only two in the Bazaar, one was the crown jewel in Mr. Akaoui's collection of textiles and was sold to King Carol of Roumania. The other belonged to Mr. Mandil's firm and was sold, if I remember correctly, to an Italian nobleman. One did see single panels from time to time, but the earlier of them, always woven in red silk and made in Bursa in the sixteenth and seventeenth centuries, were quite rare. The later examples, woven in red and green silk in the eighteenth or nineteenth centuries in Scutari, appeared more frequently. Today if a tourist in Istanbul wishes to see a fine velvet he should not lose his time in the Bazaar but go directly to the Seraglio Museum where splendid examples are on display.

Floral design on an eighteenth-century Persian brocade.

As for myself, I never bought an antique Turkish velvet in Turkey. I did buy a collection of seventeen pieces of the finest old Turkish velvets from the Kelekian estate in New York in 1947. They had all come from Constantinople several generations ago, and I presented them to the Art Institute of

Chicago where, from time to time, examples are on public display. Why did I buy in New York and not in Turkey? A Turkish proverb aptly provides the answer: "A stone is heaviest in its own place."

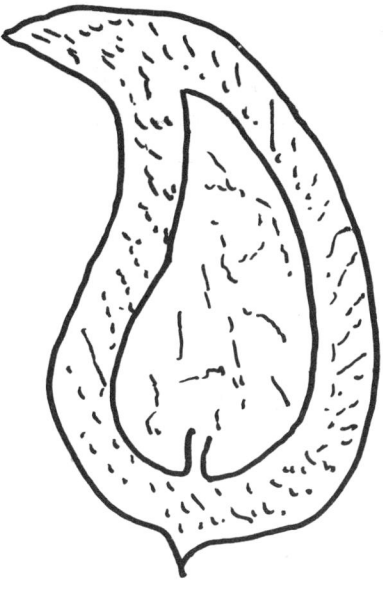

Design on a nineteenth-century Turkish brocade.

Rugs, Carpets, Brocades, and Velvets

Plates for Chapter III

All objects are in private collections unless indicated otherwise.

		Page
28.	A seventeenth-century Kula prayer rug.	81
29.	A seventeenth-century Ghordes prayer rug.	82
30.	An eighteenth-century Ghordes prayer rug.	83
31.	A seventeenth-century Transylvania prayer rug.	84
32.	A young amateur shows his prize won from the Bazaar—a magnificent antique Bergama prayer rug. (BYB-1942.)	85
33.	A silk rug woven on the looms of Sadullah, Levi & Mandil of Istanbul in 1927. There are 225 knots to the square centimeter.	86
34.	A seventeenth-century double panel of Turkish velvet made in Bursa and used in 1938 as a wall hanging in the living room of an apartment in Athens. Below it is an eighteenth-century inlaid Turkish chest and on top of this is a collection of eighteenth-century Turkish copper-gilt household objects. On the floor is a seventeenth-century dragon Kuba rug. The velvet is now in the Art Institute of Chicago and the rug at Colonial Williamsburg, Virginia.	87
35.	A seventeenth-century panel of Bursa velvet now in the Art Institute of Chicago.	88

IV

Old Silver

The finest Turkish silver seen in the Bazaar in my time was made in either Istanbul in the eighteenth century for the Imperial family and the local aristocracy or in Izmir, which was the home of many rich Levantine families of European ancestry whose business was shipping and commerce. The Istanbul products were braziers, candelabra, lanterns, mirrors, ewers, and basins, as well as all manner of small hollow objects, and flat silver ware. The Izmir objects were likely to be trays, tea and coffee services, spoon holders, jam jars, and flat table silver. The trays deserve particular attention as, whether circular, oval, or rectangular, they were always beautiful. The bottom was a plain silver sheet with a rim around it about one and one half inches high made of a band in openwork in high relief of grape leaves, vines, and fruit. The top of the rim was normally decorated with a flat band about one half inch wide in the dart and egg pattern. The two handles were cast in the form of confronted eagle heads. The design was very handsome and popular and having such a tray was apparently a matter of prestige for every European family living in Izmir. The same design, adapted to the needs of the subject, was used in making spoon holders, covered jam jars, coffee cups, or zarfs as they were called in Turkey, and other hollowware objects.

It seems appropriate to include a little story here taken from a letter that I wrote to Mr. Shaw about a special type of zarf which was rarely seen in the Bazaar even forty years ago. "You ask what IT is," said my Turkish friend. "That is difficult to answer because to a materialist IT is one thing and to a Turk of my generation IT is quite another. If I answer you in the blunt language that is the fashion in my country today—in the language of the materialist—I shall be obliged to say that IT is only an old coffee cup whose

Silver fluted zarf or coffee cup. Eighteenth century, Turkish.

usefulness has been impaired by someone's action in drilling a hole in the bottom and through it attaching a small silver filagree sphere with a hinged top. In other words IT is a piece of rubbish. But to answer your question in the manner of my choice, and in a way that I think and hope that you will understand, I call IT the jewel that fulfills all desire. Yes, that is ITS proper name and description, THE JEWEL THAT FULFILLS ALL DESIRE.

"But you are looking at the cup much too intently, Mr. Berry. Is it because my description surprises you? Take the cup into your hand. Now if you wish to see it well—to really feel its beauty—you must look at it with dreamy eyes. Let your thoughts wander as your fingers caress its lips. Try and forget that the porcelain is old Saxe, that the silver filagree is of the finest, and that the pearl is authentic. All these factors are unimportant when weighed against the real worth of the cup. That quality—its real value—rests upon subtle associations growing out of precious and intimate moments in the lives of its owners—recollections of hours filled with peace and tranquility—souvenirs of a life in an earthly paradise...

"But I see that I am not making progress in informing you about the cup and also I see that I shall have to be more explicit in order to be understood by a young man of this generation. Perhaps I can make my task easier by telling you a bit about myself. Then maybe you will understand. At least I believe that you will.

"During my early manhood I was an official in the War Ministry in Stanbul. Habitually I left my desk in the afternoon and was rowed over here to Scutari by one of my men. From the landing stage I always walked directly to the selamlik of my house where a servant helped me to remove my Stambouli and my shoes. My man assisted me into a loose-fitting burnous and comfortable slippers. Then I would stretch out, half-reclining and half-sitting, on this sofa here by the window. Sometimes my fingers would be busy with a tesbih, but more often I took this cup from its place on a shelf beside a window and toyed with it as I watched the sea. The cup belonged to my father and perhaps to his father, but for the latter I am not certain. In my father's time people believed that a small piece of amber placed in a cup of coffee gave the drinker increased genetic power. Amber was used thus throughout the land, and cups similar to this one, were made specially so as to confine the amber while permitting its strength to mix with the coffee. Everyone associated such cups with unusual powers and, indeed, this cup has come to have such a significance to me. Each evening as I sat by the window and caressed it, little by little I would shake off the cares of the day. My nerves would quiet down and my mind would reach a state of repose. All reverberations of the clash and clamor of the life which I experienced throughout the day on the other side of the Bosphorus would leave me and eventually I would feel at peace with the world. Then I would clap my hands together in order to command a servant to prepare coffee. After sipping it, if I felt a desire for companionship, I was ready to enter the harem....

"Do you understand now, Mr. Berry, why I told you that the physical features of the cup do not determine its value?"

After each meal in a typical eighteenth or nineteenth century home of a person of wealth in the Ottoman Empire, two servants, one carrying an ewer, and the other a basin and an embroidered towel, passed around the dining table from guest to guest. Water was poured from the ewer over the hands of each guest into the basin, and the hands dried with the towel. Often an incense burner was presented with its fumes assisting in the drying, and then a few drops of rose water from a sprinkler were dropped on the finger tips. It will be well understood that cleaning the hands was an essential part of dining when one recalls that most food was eaten with the fingers, often being taken from a common bowl. The finest ewers and basins were essentially the same, some plain and others fluted, but all about eighteen inches high, made of sterling silver, and very graceful in line.

Another type of silver object found in the Bazaar was the grandfather of our modern fountain pens. It was called a devit, and in fact was a portable ink pot with case attached for quill pens. It was constructed with a hollow rectangular shaft from eight to fourteen inches long for holding quills or reeds. Each end of the shaft was decorated with engravings. One end was hinged to open, the other permanently closed. Attached to the shaft was a keg-shaped receptacle with a hinged cover. In this there was a ball of cotton thread that was kept saturated with ink. When a quill was pushed into the ball of thread enough ink adhered to it for writing purposes. A devit was carried in the folds of the sash of a scribe much as a dagger was carried in the folds of the sash of many another person.

The lanterns, bird cages, braziers, and candlesticks were made on order for the Palace and its dependencies. Accordingly, the best workmanship went into their manufacture. They may be taken as the finest examples of Turkish eighteenth and nineteenth century craftsmanship rather than as representative examples. Today, the tourist can see fine specimens of these works in the Seraglio Museum in Istanbul. In the late 1920s he could very often see examples being offered for sale in the Bazaar by the heirs of the person who had received them as gifts from the reigning Sultan. The lantern illustrated, according to the inscription engraved upon it, was given to Ussuf Ezzettin Effendi by his father, Sultan Abdul Aziz, as a part of the Prince's dowry upon the occasion of his marriage in 1867. At that time, of course, Istanbul streets were not lighted, or were, at best, very poorly lighted. Anyone venturing out after sunset was accompanied by servants carrying lanterns. The lanterns of the rich were of silver, or copper plated with gold.

The Turkish hand mirrors were about eighteen inches in diameter, usually circular but occasionally oval, and nearly always without a handle, being held by a servant when in use. The glass was kept in place by a narrow scalloped frame of engraved silver. When not in use the mirror was placed glass downward on a table. The top side of the mirror was highly decorated in repoussé work, sometimes gilded, in a design of scrolls, ribbons, garlands, flowers, and leaves. The top side is slightly convex to show its beauty to advantage as it rests on a table.

Antique silver objects, usually Byzantine but occasionally Roman or earlier, in the form of jewelry, spoons, and, more rarely, vessels, would turn up from time to time in the Bazaar. From 1928 onward there was much Imperial Russian silver in the Istanbul Bazaar, it being what the refugees, following the Bolshevik Revolution, brought with them and sold piece by piece. Some of it, samovars, tea services, and such, was strikingly beautiful. In the winter of 1929, Mrs. William Boyce Thompson of Philadelphia called on her yacht, the *S.S. Savonarola*, at Istanbul. Mrs. Thompson was passionately fond of old silver and on her visit she practically bought out the stock of the Merinsky brothers which, in terms of dollars, was the largest Bazaar sale that I had known. On that occasion the Turkish nation lost a lot of silver metal, but it later got a yacht at a bargain price, buying the *Savonarola* as a gift to Ataturk from a grateful nation. The yacht, still as beautiful as a dream, remains today the Turkish presidential yacht.

Two varieties of silver spoons. First century B.C., Roman.

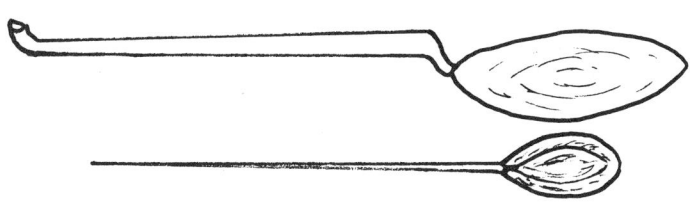

Two other varieties of silver spoons. First century B.C., Roman.

Old Silver

Small boxes, known in the Bazaar as Turkish snuff boxes, were available in quantity in the late 1920s and 1930s. "What does the bear understand of the flute?" runs a Turkish proverb. "And what does the world know about Turkish snuff boxes?" Elea once said to me when I pressed him for information about a snuff box. Certainly, anyone will agree, there is a great deal to learn about snuff boxes and a great deal to unlearn as well!

The old Turkish boxes, which, as a matter of fact, are as often purses or reliquaries as snuff boxes, are seldom of sterling silver and almost never quite as old as their Bazaar owners make them out to be. And, even accepting the fact that they were made within the boundaries of the Ottoman Empire, no one will claim that they are all Turkish. They are, however, boxes; usually boxes, I hastily add, for in the Bazaar I have seen a transformed English watch case passed off as a snuff box of rare and unusual form! But they were very attractive, and inexpensive, and of silver, often low grade, but sometimes sterling. Occasionally they bore a government control. The controls took the form of a toura, or monogram of the Sultan reigning at the time that the box was made, or taken to the assay office for stamping. In addition to the toura, from the time of the reign of Sultan Abdul Hamid, a Turkish word, *saf*, meaning pure, was often used with the toura but on a separate die. A control is useful in dating an object, and is a guarantee of the quality of the silver, 900 in Turkey.

The Moslem boxes were, like the embroidered towels, ornamented with a floral spray or garden scene. Simple floral sprays were popular throughout the Moslem world as flowers were appreciated for their beauty and fragrance and they were symbolic of youth and freshness. Merinsky once told me that it was possible to tell the approximate age of the person for whom a box had been ordered by looking at the flowers that ornamented the box; a rose bud indicating youth and full blown rose maturity. In many boxes the flower motif is expanded into a garden scene. The garden in all Moslem lands suggests peace and repose, just as the hunting scene suggests combat and action. It is not strange, therefore, that many boxes that were made to contain powders which were conducive to repose and relaxation should be ornamented with garden scenes. Sometimes the garden is surrounded by walls, or is on an island, a suggestion which conveys the thought of isolation, quiet, and repose. Another popular design for Moslem boxes was the shell. This motif is supposed to have made its first appearance in Moslem art in Istanbul in the decoration of the Chinili Kiosk, the first Moslem palace built after the conquest of the city by Mehmet II in 1453. Just when the shell was first used in the ornamentation of a silver box I do not know, but it is found in simple form on some of the oldest boxes that have come down to us. It appears on later boxes together with flowers and ribbons, and on still later ones as a secondary feature. The significance of the shell in Turkish art is not clear. I was told on one occasion that the small silver boxes decorated with shells were once popular as gifts from gentlemen to ladies. Venus, according to an Eastern legend, sprang from a shell, and as the shell of every Turkish box is open, one can assume that the shell without its Venus is a subtle compliment to the lady recipient and she is, herself, Venus in the eyes of the giver. It is a pretty fiction that fits nicely into the romantic conception of courtship in bygone times.

Silver cup. First century B.C., *Roman.*

Most of the Christian boxes contain a hint in their decoration that they were made for someone of the Greek Orthodox faith. The decoration tells a story and often indicates clearly whether the box was made for religious or laical purposes. Occasionally I saw a box in the Bazaar which was made for conveying holy bread from the Church to the bedside of the dying in order to administer the last sacrament. There are a number of small perforations to admit air in the bottom of such a box. On the cover a chalice, covered by a veil held by two doves is pictured in repoussé. Over all is a canopy, like the canopies that cover the altars of Greek Orthodox churches. One nineteenth-century box I have seen was decorated with a picture of the story of St. George and the dragon. The story, judging from the number of old ikons that one sees illustrating it, has been popular for centuries among Christian peoples of the Near East. To us today the legend may appear to be only a delightful bit of folklore, but it, together with similar legends, had a tremendous impact for generations upon the minds of the Christian people of Asia Minor. It is, therefore, more than a picture worked in silver on an old box. It is a demonstration of the influence that the teachings of the Church had on the individual who ordered the box and who presumably was representative of the time in which he lived.

Another silver reliquary that I found was embossed with the child Jesus in the arms of the Virgin, the subject in all probability copied from a popular ikon of the time. To the left and the right of the head are, in Greek letters "Mother of God" and "Son." This box is stamped with the toura of Sultan Selim III (1789-1807). In view of the decoration, these boxes may be classified as ecclesiastical, but Orthodox secular boxes were also made, and in greater number if the number of those surviving is a test of the quantity produced. One such, stamped with the toura of Sultan Abdul Medjid (1839-1867), is decorated appropriately for a marriage or betrothal gift. Homing pigeons, supporting a wedding ring, form the central motif and below it two hearts beat in unison, symbolic of a happy union.

Other boxes, highly decorated with floral elements and occasionally inconspicuously with some form of animal life, are not easily classified as Moslem or Christian. Strictly applied, the reproduction of figures representing human or animal life was forbidden to Moslems. But two hundred years ago d'Ohsson remarked that the interdiction was not absolute. He noted that when the figures were small they were tolerated. No Moslem refused to accept a gold coin from a Christian country because there was a head stamped on the coin, and nobody refused to own a carpet on which was woven the tree of life, a popular Moslem motif, because there was a bird resting on a branch of the tree. In fact some forms of animal life are not only tolerated but are venerated by all Moslems. All alike respect pigeons, for was it not a pair of pigeons that once saved the Prophet from death by his pursuers? And then there was Kitmir, the canine companion of the Seven Sleepers, who is vouchsafed a place in paradise.

While by association the holiness of these animals is accepted by all Moslems, certain Moslem sects countenance the reproduction of likenesses of other animals. The Sheites, for example, turned a deaf ear for centuries to warnings of the theologians against the reproduction of animals in decorative arts, and some Sunni groups, the Becktashis, for one, place a liberal interpretation on this particular section of the Koran. Thus, the presence of inconspicuous animals incorporated in the decoration of snuff boxes does not furnish sufficiently strong evidence for stating that the boxes are of Christian origin.

Occasionally there is an inscription engraved, or inlaid with gold or silver, on a metal object and these are usually interesting. Once I bought in the Bazaar one of those yard-long Oriental sabers with a

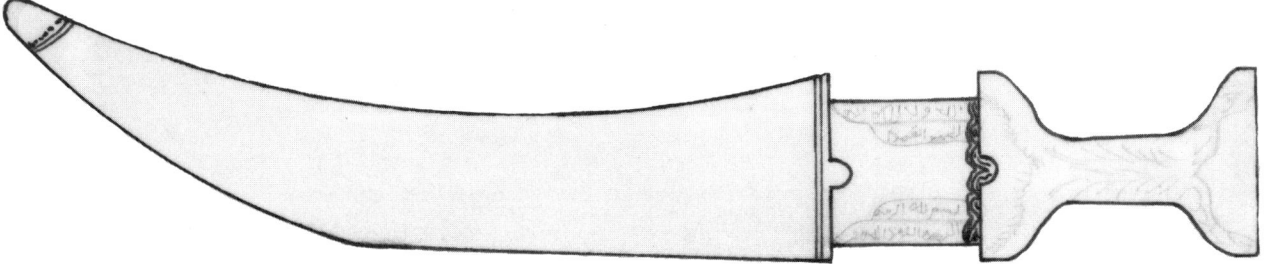

Turkish officer's dagger with silver gilt scabbard and handle, damascened steel blade with gold inlaid inscription. Nineteenth century.

curved blade and silver scabbard. The bone handle was shaped like elephant ears. It was not a thing of beauty but I liked it, perhaps influenced by the sales talk of the merchant, one of the Macedonian brothers. In showing it to me he argued fervently that while the saber *might* not be a lovely thing in everybody's eyes it was of such great practical value that I should not fail to purchase it. He said that as a piece of desk equipment it would be ideal for use as a paper knife for opening my letters! I could not resist this logic so I bought the saber and, as there was some beautiful writing in gold inlaid on the blade, I asked Ali Nadji Bey to translate it. He read it: "Made by Abdullah in the year 1226 for the owner, Ahmed Agha, who, upon seizing this sword, said passionately, 'Oh God! sing the praises of God. By the grace of God may the gates of his favor be opened to me! By his favor may this knife be full of success so that both worlds may be gained by its owner!' " Well, now, that's a prayer, I thought.

As with the embroideries, friends often asked me to advise them when an attractive piece of old Turkish silver came on the market. Even after I left Turkey some of them continued to ask me to keep a sharp eye open for fine examples of old Turkish silver. This was really quite a reasonable request as in the capitals of the successor states of the Ottoman Empire there was much beautiful silver to be found that had come from Istanbul. Mr. Mandil, for one, had for years wanted to have a silver lantern and, not having succeeded in getting one, had enlisted my aid. The following is a letter I wrote to him from Cairo in 1938.

Dear Mr. Mandil:

If I had not been in Persia you would have had by now the silver lantern that you want so much. But, because I recall so vividly a Persian experience, you will have to wait for a lantern until another sort of opportunity presents itself. This is the story: To celebrate the anniversary of the Prophet's birth, the Governor of Cairo gave a huge party. At the party I was standing beside a local prince and to make conversation I told him that I was looking for a silver lantern and a silver birdcage for a friend who lived in Turkey. In spite of searching high and low, I told him, I had found none.

"But you have kismet (luck)," the Prince said, and then, seeing by my expression that I did not understand his meaning, added, "In my country palace on the Bosphorus I have several old silver lanterns and birdcages and you shall have your choice of them. They were my grandmother's. The birdcages have not been used since the old lady died and we ceased going to Istanbul in the summer. The lanterns we put away when electric torches came into general use. I offer to you as a *gift* such of them as may please you."

Doubtless you are wondering what this all has to do with Persia and I shall tell you just now. A Persian aristocrat who had read one of my published articles asked me one day when I was in Teheran to call on him in his garden and see his collection of Persian art. I went gladly but my feelings quickly changed as there was spread out before me such a collection of monstrosities, such a conglomeration of objects in bad taste, that I was simply horrified. Desperately I looked around for something to praise and hastily chose a fragment of a nineteenth century Persian brocaded vest as being among the least offensive. It was coarse in workmanship and gaudy in color, the sort of thing that a merchant in the Bazaar in a benevolent mood might buy for ten dollars. Nevertheless, it was the best thing in sight and I am afraid that in my panic I praised it immoderately. At any rate before I left the garden my host offered the vest to me as a gift! But I firmly declined to accept it saying that as I was soon to leave Persia for my home in America, I would not have the occasion in the few days that remained before my departure to show my appreciation in a fitting manner.

"But that doesn't matter," my host said, "from your home you can send me one of those cheap American automobiles."

And so, Mr. Mandil, you will have to wait for a lantern until I can *buy* one!

Plates for Chapter IV

The silver objects shown on the following plates all came out of the Grand Bazaar in Istanbul. When photographed many years ago they were the property of friends. Similar pieces can be seen today in the Seraglio Museum of Istanbul.

Page

36. 1. Nineteenth-century fluted sterling silver ewer and basin, Constantinople. 97
    2. Nineteenth-century silver repoussé mirror, Constantinople.
    3. Nineteenth-century silver repoussé mirror, Constantinople.
    4. Nineteenth-century plain silver ewer and basin, Constantinople.

37. 1. Eighteenth-century sterling silver devit, Constantinople. 98
    2. Nineteenth-century silver coffee pot with ivory handle, Constantinople.
    3. Eighteenth-century silver water cup, Constantinople.
    4. Nineteenth-century silver dervish cup, ornamented with niello, Van.
    5. Nineteenth-century silver tea tray, Smyrna.
    6. Nineteenth-century engine-turned silver sherbet tray, Constantinople.

Small silver boxes from the Grand Bazaar bought in the 1920s and 1930s:

38. 1. Eighteenth-century sacramental box of the Greek Orthodox church. 99
    2. Seventeenth-century box with St. George and the dragon on the cover.
    3. Seventeenth-century reliquary box with picture of Virgin and Child on cover.
    4. Secular Orthodox silver box made in 1840.
    5. Eighteenth-century box with cover decorated with an arabesque design with a bird in the center.
    6. Late-sixteenth-century silver box with a shell design on the cover.
    7. Eighteenth-century box with a cover design of shell and garland.
    8. Nineteenth-century silver box with a coat of arms and shell decoration on the cover.
    9. A box with flowering plant motif dating about 1780. The arches suggest a garden scene.
    10. A popular Moslem flower spray decoration was used on the cover of this box dating from the late seventeenth century.
    11. The cover of this eighteenth-century box shows a walled city enclosed in scrolls.

39. The plate shows a table in an Istanbul apartment in 1930 decorated with old silver objects from the Bazaar. Behind it is a mirror, and on the table are coffee pots, devits, a sefertas (silver compartmented portable lunch basket), and minor objects. The wall picture is an engraving of St. Sophia by Fossati published in 1852. 100

40. A sterling silver street lantern made in Constantinople in 1867 on order by Sultan Abdul Aziz for his son and heir Yusuf Ezzettin Effendi. It stands on a carved eighteenth-century money chest that came from a Hamam. On the wall is an engraving by Pretozzi. 101

1

2

3

4

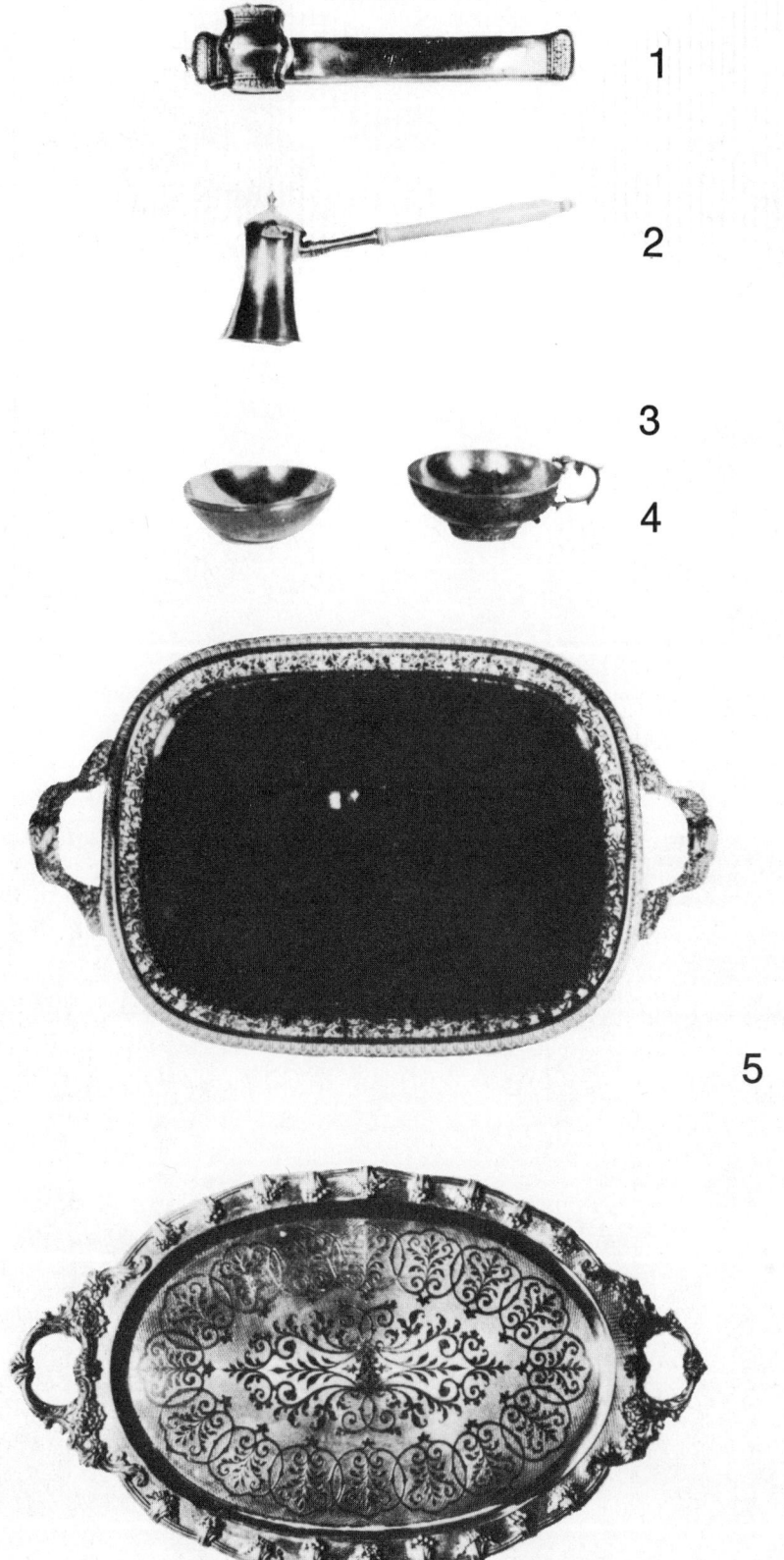

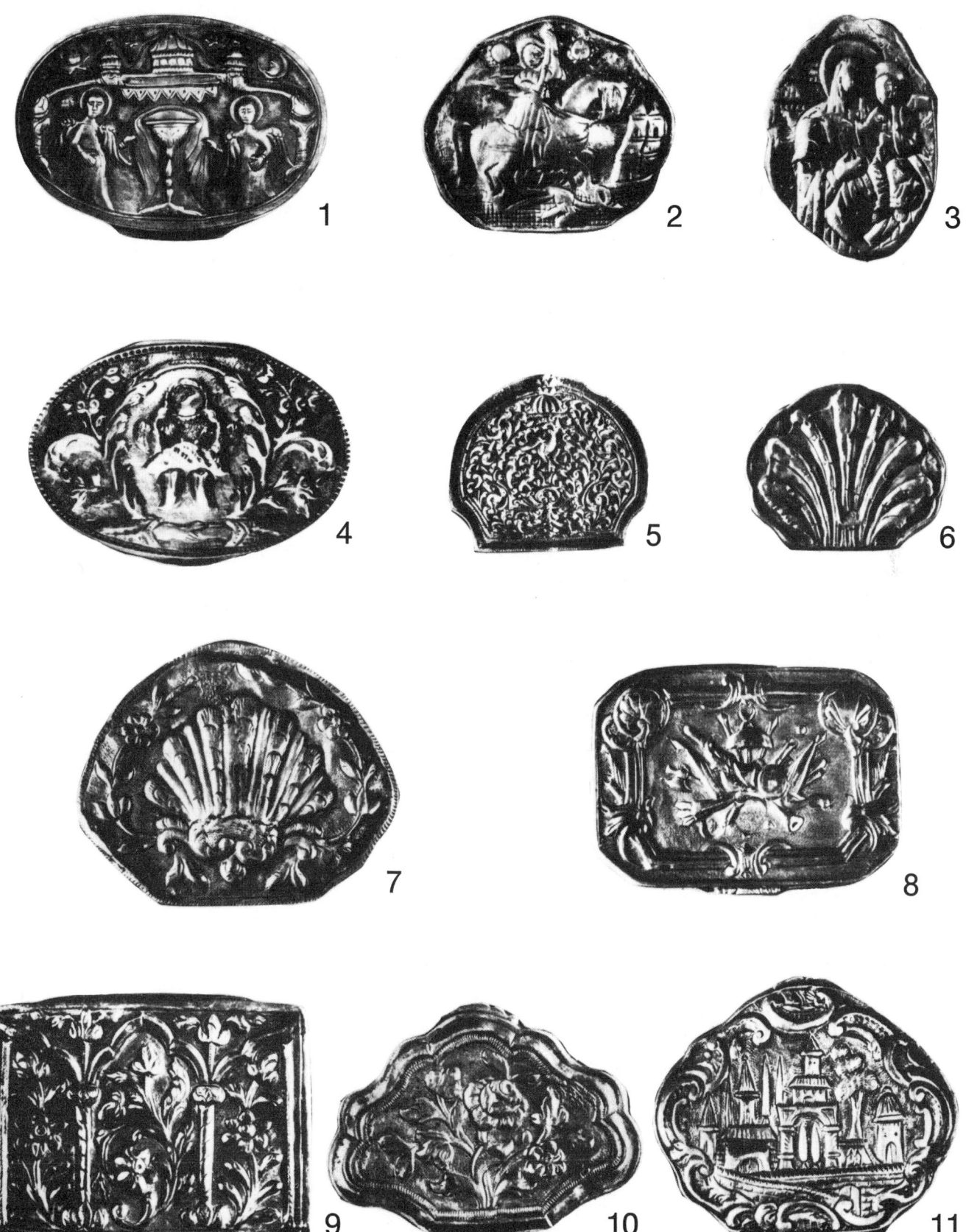

V

Bronzes

One day, when we were just beginning to realize the full impact of the economic depression of the 1930s, Bill Cramp said to me, "We must move with the times. We must lower our sights from silver to bronze. Today we will play a new game. After work this afternoon we will go to the Bazaar together, separate at the entrance, and meet at Mandil's at closing time. You look around and choose a new item to collect. It must be antique, interesting, beautiful, and not cost more than a dollar at the most. I will do the same. The better selection wins supper." That afternoon I bought my first door disc. When Cramp saw it he said that it certainly qualified as costing less than a dollar, but it failed when it came to beauty or interest. I thought I had lost a supper until it developed that he had bought nothing because he was stopped by the dollar ceiling. And so, by default I began to look in the Bazaar for door discs and after a while even found them interesting and sometimes beautiful.

"But what in the world is a door disc? Couldn't you buy something useful?" asked Betty Carp when she heard the news. And the explanations started. Old Turkish doors did not have spring locks or door knobs. They were bolted from within to close securely. To open and close when unbolted each had a large iron or bronze ring, placed where we place a doorknob, held in place by a huge staple of the same material and backed by a disc which protected the wood of the door from the blow when the ring was released. These discs were what were called door discs. The simplest ones were plain discs of iron. The more ornate discs were of copper cut by or cast with intricately designed perforations in some beautiful geometric design. The metal was engraved in a pattern of flowers, vines, and leaves, all plated with gold, and backed with red velvet to show the perforations of the design advantageously. Between these two extremes many variations were found. The discs varied in size from an inch in diameter (for one made for a cabinet) to ten inches in diameter (for the principal door of an Imperial mosque).

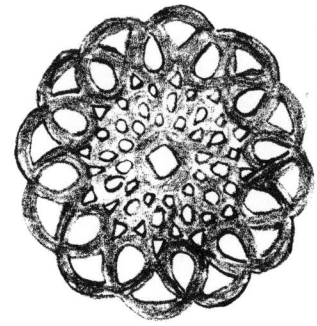

Turkish seventeenth-century door disc. Copper gilt.

Turkish doors offered promises of things hidden, and so they were often very beautiful. This of course applied particularly to the inner doors in houses, and the great doors of the Imperial mosques leading from the courtyard into the mosque, the doors of wall cabinets in kiosks, and even to chests. The basic door frame was of seasoned wood, often oak. Over this was inlaid a geometric design made with pieces of tortoise shell, mother-of-pearl, silver, and rare woods of various colors. The metal door furnishings were of copper or bronze, gold plated, perforated, and engraved to harmonize with the door decoration. The discs, as indicated, were a minor part of the metal furnishings.

It was the pastime of a few afternoons to assemble examples of all of the varieties of discs available in the Bazaar, but only then did the real work begin. First, I visited every Imperial mosque and its dependencies in the city to see various types of discs in their original position. This way I could accurately fix the dating of these types. These visits were never a source of material but were always a source of information. Then I visited the various Palace-Museums of the city, and finally the yalis and kiosks in the environs that had as yet not been touched by the craze of moderization that was sweeping the country. Finally I searched the bookstores and libraries for old books illustrated with drawings of the doors of the time. Then it was back to the Bazaar for material, or tips as to where I might find material. Occasionally a merchant would tell me of an eighteenth- or nineteenth-century house that was being torn down to make room for an apartment building where I might find some door discs. On two occasions I was advised of seventeenth-century buildings, one a bath and the other a school of no historic importance, that were being demolished to widen a street. I followed both tips to the source and in each case was rewarded for my efforts. At both I got several good discs and at the bath some splendid tile fragments that had once been the mirror plate of a fountain. Henceforth I was on the alert for tile fragments when searching for discs in old buildings. The tiles that I found were from panels that had been used in the ornamentation of mosques, palaces, and fountains. For the most part they were broken sections but sufficiently large to indicate the pattern and always well enough preserved to show the splendid colors and painting. My pleasure was in finding and studying, and when that was done I was glad to pass on the collection to somebody to whom it would be useful. At about this time Dr. Mehmet Agaoglu, former curator of the Efkaf Museum in Istanbul, had gone to America to set up a program of Islamic studies at the University of Michigan. I asked him if he would care to have my tiles as a gift for his classroom work, and he accepted gladly. Then I asked Howard Elting, who was going to America by ship from Istanbul on his first home leave, if he would take them. He, too, accepted but probably not so gladly for even I was shocked by the bulk and weight of the tiles when packed. But they arrived safely and Dr. Agaoglu, Elting, and I each probably derived some profit out of the experience. Thereafter, whenever a colleague at a foreign post started to ask me to carry something home for him, I would interrupt with a bright smile and say emphatically, "Certainly, anything that you can put into an envelope."

The morale of everybody during those days of financial readjustment was more or less affected, and good humor and a tolerant attitude were often replaced by remarks with a sharp edge. Of course, a collection of such objects as door discs provided many opportunities for such remarks! My escape clause, which I fell back on when all my explanations did not satisfy, was to say, "Well, of course, I do not collect door discs exclusively. There are other bronzes in the Bazaar." And when the time arrived that I was collecting delightful little bronze figurines, some thousands of years old, I became almost respectable in the eyes of many of my critics, while others gave a sort of a left-handed approval of a door disc collection by saying: "At least you cannot waste much money on door discs." I agreed. I continued a sporadic interest in door discs until I gave my collection to the Art Institute of Chicago. This was long after Cramp's departure from Istanbul, where he was remembered with approval by the local people whom we had interviewed together on the subject of discs. One such mosque guardian, meeting me by chance several years later, asked, "And where is your friend?" I said, perhaps unconsciously a little sadly, that he had gone to Belize. The man replied, "Too bad. He was young." And I wondered if the old Turk's understanding of the whereabouts of Cramp's domicile, and Cramp's own feeling toward it, did not have more than a little in common.

The Bazaar was full of other bronzes. Mrs. Lewis Heck, for one, collected candlesticks, because, she once explained to me, each candlestick had its own personality. She was quite right. All the Bazaar

Bronze bull. Eighth to seventh century B.C.

candlesticks were antique by American standards and some were even venerable. In the first category were the dozens of single candlesticks, mostly different and each made for a bedside night table. Then came the pairs made for ornamenting chimneys. Finally, were the candelabra for the entrance halls and

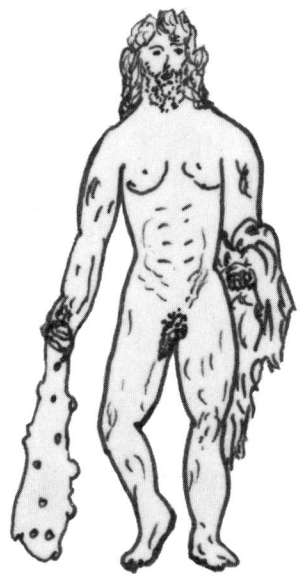

Statuette of Heracles. Roman.

Bronzes

dining rooms of great houses. Among the venerable were the floor candlesticks that were made just the right height for the light of the flame to fall on the pages of the Koran as a Mullah sat crosslegged on the floor of a mosque and read his Koran by candlelight. Then there came, in pairs and double pairs, candlesticks in fine straight shafts, nearly as high as a man, that once had stood around the catafalques in Turkish tombs. Finally, there were the huge brass candlesticks, each weighing a hundred pounds or more, that had stood one on each side of the mirab in every mosque of importance. They were all there in the Bazaar to choose from in various sizes, shapes, metals, and prices.

With the candlesticks were collapsible copper lanterns in various sizes, each with a beautifully perforated top and bottom joined by a parchment that folded accordionlike. There were mortars and pestles that once belonged to metal workers, pharmacists, or cooks. There were great trays of copper; the Turkish ones relatively simply decorated with engraved floral motifs and the Persian intricately carved, made to serve for diningroom tables or to display Oriental pastries in confectioners' shops. There were also great copper kraters for holding sherbets, bowls, ewers with their basins, and cooking and serving vessels. One day while trying to buy one of these bowls, I lost the bowl but learned a lesson that often served me well thereafter. This bowl was displayed with other things in a shop that sold sweets in a large village. I asked the price and the owner shrugged his shoulders, which usually means "you offer a price"; I offered fifty liras which was refused. I gradually raised my offer to one hundred liras, which was about the maximum price that such a bowl would bring at a good antique shop in Istanbul. When this sum was refused I decided, just to see the owner's idea of the bowl's value, to ask him if he would accept two hundred liras for the bowl. He replied, "The money of the infidel is not good for the faithful." Thus it was, in a village, that I learned the answer to give the beggars in Istanbul, who, in 1928 and until the reforms of Ataturk introduced changed mores, beseeched money wherever and whenever crowds gathered.

Here I would like to digress a moment and tell of one such beggar I tried to make over into a businessman. In a letter to Mr. Shaw I wrote:

"A fortnight ago on my way to the Bazaar I was asked for some money by one of the vagabond boys of Galata. You know, I am sure, the type of young vagabond who begs at the Tunnel entrance during rush hours and gambles under the Galata bridge while other people work. I suggested that, if he wanted money, he might follow my example and work for it. He expressed his willingness to try the experiment and so together we went to the 'Bit Bazaar' in search of business opportunities. What looked to me to be such an opportunity, Mehmed, for that he said was his name, uncovered in the form of an old portable shoe polishing outfit. I bought it together with a collection of slightly caked polishes for four liras (two dollars) and presented it to Mehmed with my sincere wishes for his future prosperity.

"About a week later I happened on to my protégé and, hesitating a moment in order to think of a phrase for waving aside the effusive thanks and lavish compliments with which I expected to be showered, greeted him and asked how he found his new outfit. 'I wish that you would buy me another,' he said pouting. 'This one is no good. The cash drawer is too small.' I thought, 'Here is a boy with a practical eye. He will succeed in business when given a chance.' "

Among the most beautiful of the more expensive coppers were the services of Yaldiz ware. These were fashionable in the eighteenth century. They were of copper heavily plated with gold so that they resembled the solid gold services that were used in the Palace in more prosperous eras. A tray, engraved in a simple floral motif, a single jam jar, with similar decoration, or a covered dish for pilaf, were frequently to be found but sets of these were quite rare.

One afternoon at Salih's I saw a splendid complete service of Yaldiz consisting of a tray about a yard in diameter, a tall covered compote bowl in the center, and six smaller and lower covered dishes around it. Every vessel was in excellent condition and the ancient mercury gilding perfect. In my mind I could not find one fault to mention as an opener in bargaining for the set, so, after looking at it in silent admiration for a few minutes, I said, "Too bad the jam jars are missing!" Salih, who was in a fine humor that day, probably having just made a good sale, replied, "Yes, but leave the set, Mr. Berry, and wait several weeks. It is still winter and although the season for lambing, it is not yet the time for jam jars." I must have looked puzzled for Salih asked me if I did not know the Nasreddin Hoja story. I shook my head and he continued, "One day the Hoja asked a neighbor for the loan of one of his largest saucepans. The neighbor agreed and Nasreddin took the pan home. After some weeks the neighbor asked for its return.

"Not yet," the Hoja told him, "it has just given birth to young and it is not yet well enough to be moved." The man went away in amazement as he had never before heard of saucepans giving birth to young. Soon, to his astonishment, the saucepan and a tiny one were given to him with a note from the Hoja stating that the little one was the pick of the litter. The following year Nasreddin was asked to accept the loan of the large saucepan. The Hoja willingly did so, and as the neighbor heard nothing further of it he went after a month's time to Nasreddin and asked news of his saucepan. "Alas, your saucepan is dead!" said Nasreddin. "Dead!" replied the neighbor. "You know very well, you rascal, that saucepans do not die." "But they do," put in Nasreddin, "just as surely as they have young!"

Salih had made his point and I carried home the Yaldiz set agreeing to pay for it in monthly installments. It was really a prize and it has graced a large living room table in my Bosphorus villa for years. Guests often remark it and more than one acquisitive woman has hinted broadly that she would like to carry away just one of the dishes as a souvenir since I had so many! At a cocktail party I was rescued from one such person, who was becoming unusually insistent by a Turkish friend who told another Nasreddin Hoja story. My friend said to the woman, "Mr. Berry is a collector and collectors are very much like preachers; there are some words they simply do not understand. I will illustrate what I mean with a story from one of our local folklore heroes, Nasreddin Hoja. One day the Hoja coming onto a pond saw a group of men, shouting and gesticulating, clustered close to the water's edge. He approached and noted that they were trying to rescue a fellow Hoja, or preacher, who had fallen into the pond. The preacher was certainly drowning and the people on the bank were shouting all sorts of instructions to him. 'Give a hand. Give us your hand,' many shouted, but the preacher paid no heed to them. Nasreddin pressed through the crowd saying 'Let me attend to him.' He came to the edge of the water and calmly said to the drowning Hoja, 'Take my hand.' Immediately the man grasped Nasreddin's hand and was pulled from the water. The crowd stood stupefied by this bit of magic and Nasreddin, noting their surprise, explained, 'The preacher has not the habit of giving but he understands taking!'"

The archaeological antiques found in the Istanbul Bazaars in the early 1930s, or those that merited the name and the price of antiques, were, as I have indicated, concentrated in the shops of the two principal dealers or their successors. But nearly every stall in the Bedestan had some minor archaeological objects to show the customer. These were usually junk, bought at the price of junk by the dealers with the hope of selling at the price of antiques. Indeed, if one of these Bedestan dealers in the 1930s happened to buy an archaeological object of value he quickly hastened to sell it to George or Hagop.

Among the archaeological bronzes to be found in the Bazaars were weapons from all ages of history, prehistoric to late Ottoman; jewelry in bronze of the humbler classes of earlier civilizations, such as finger rings, earrings, safety pins and straight pins, and necklaces and bracelets such as women and men in their social environment might wear to hold their clothes together and keep their egos satisfactorily inflated.

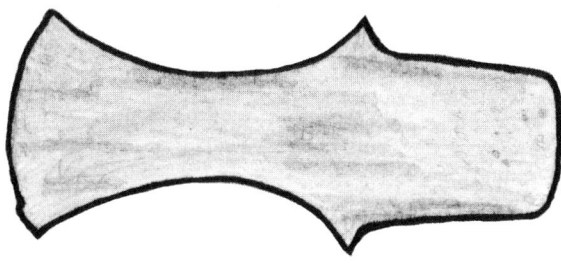

Ax. Bronze Age.

Authentic prehistoric axes, Roman surgical instruments, Byzantine crosses, and small statuettes, either votive offerings or appendages from household utensils were available in quantity. Occasionally larger statues in bronze, sometimes life size, also appeared, although seeing one was a once-in-a-year event and such important bronzes were always hidden away from the general public.

The little bronzes from the Bazaar could be grouped into at least three categories, according to the purpose for which they were made: (1) those made for personal adornment, (2) those made for the ornamentation of vessels, furniture, etc., and (3) small statuettes. All were made from cast bronze. Many examples were available from the prehistoric period, a few from the classical period, and large numbers from the Hellenistic, Roman, and Byzantine periods. Many of these objects, usually in the form of animals, were really minor works of art, but at the time they were not highly regarded because they were designated as "fragments." In one sense this designation was correct as a small cast bronze ornament could have been the handle of a large bronze caldron which was not cast but hammered out of a sheet of thin metal. A caldron rarely arrived at the Bazaar intact, but I recall one occasion when a caldron was found buried in earth and appeared to the excavators to be intact, but the heavily corroded vessel crumbled into bits as it was removed from the soil. However, the handle, rim, and foot of the vessel, being solidly cast, were recovered in near perfect condition. Each was a complete object, although they had been parts of a larger object, and in one sense of the word, each was a fragment. The statuettes, often made as votive offerings, but sometimes formerly the handles of mirrors or cooking vessels, were also, at the time of which I write, spoken of deprecatingly because they were "fragments." Furthermore, it was said that objects from more ancient times seen in the Bazaar in our time could not be valuable because of their number, or even beautiful, because they were commonplace! Such was the prevailing attitude forty years ago.

Most of the antique bronze objects that I bought in the Bazaar were really insignificant although authentic appendages of larger objects, whose interest developed as they took their appropriate place in a series of similar objects. Individually they were nothing; as a group they became a "collection" and hence of some educational value. The making of a collection was a form of creating wealth and that was always a stimulating exercise. I enjoyed examining these little artifacts of other times and occasionally buying them. They had certain distinct advantages over complete objects: they cost very little, they were not wanted by local museums or great collectors, and, for study purposes, they presented the same problems as complete major objects. Additionally, they had an appeal to me because they were of the people, not of the state, or of the king, or of God. I never tried to define my exact thoughts on this subject but there is a similar feeling in a statement by Jacques Lipchitz as quoted from the *Before Cortes* publication of the Metropolitan Museum in New York in 1970: "I also found so-called great art too pompous, too stiff. What at this time was called minor art was freer, more imaginative, more open to all kinds of unorthodox expression: all kinds of daring in the handling of materials, and I preferred to surround myself with this type of art than with the great collectors' pieces."

In the 1930s in the Bazaar, and particularly in the Bedestan, there existed a plethora of opportunities. As Hagop once said to me, "You will see what you look for" and this was certainly true in the Bedestan in those days. What you wanted was there. All that you had to do was to locate it. And what you did not know that you wanted was also there, if you looked about well. I looked about regularly as did another frequent visitor to the Bazaar, Bay Huseyin Koçabaş. If anything, Bay Huseyin's passion was greater than mine. He loved locating small objects, cleaning them, restoring them, uniting them with missing elements, and then placing them in a small private museum which he created, and which today is a monument to his industry and a credit to his country. Another person, one of my compatriots who lived in Rome, took a larger view of things. He often visited the Istanbul Bazaar in the 1950s, being called there by merchants who had something that they hoped to sell him. He had a good eye for antiquities, backed by academic training in archaeology, plus a large and growing experience. Topping all this he had great courage and daring. I recall a story he told me many years ago of an excursion that he made into the heart of Anatolia to see a large bronze. Alone, armed only with his money belt, he took a scheduled airplane from Istanbul to a provincial capital. Arriving in the late afternoon he hired a taxi to take him to the place of rendezvous some twenty miles away on a lonely country road. There he

Bronze lamp. Byzantine. Fifth to seventh century A.D.

dismissed the taxi and waited for dusk and the arrival of his escort. This man came in a jeep somewhat late and together, my compatriot knowing little Turkish and his companion no other language, they started over a track in the direction of the mountains. Two hours later when the terrain became too difficult they left the jeep and proceeded on foot. He told me that he would never forget the beauty of that walk under a full moon which flooded with mellow light the Anatolian steppe. There was no other light, no sign of life, just two men walking silently in the midst of solitude. He returned to Istanbul safely the following day and I, for one, was filled with admiration for his courage.

Studded bronze fibulae or safety pin. Eighth century B.C.

I never bought a major bronze, marble, or silver antiquity in an Eastern Mediterranean country, although many were offered to me, because I felt that such objects belonged in the museums of the country where they were found. The local authorities at the time that I was an active collector were aware of my attitude, and appreciated it, and, perhaps because of it, were very helpful to me in learning about and buying bronze artifacts, old coins, and elements of jewelry, objects that were mass-produced in antiquity and of which examples existed in local museums in quantity and of a quality that often was superior to what I possessed.

While I never regretted my policy in purchasing objects, I learned over the time to be slow in passing judgment on people who acted differently from me. I was influenced in this direction by the fact that I knew of several instances where large bronze statues were melted for their metal value by the finders and large marbles were burnt for lime because they could not be sold as antiquities. It is true that these were of secondary quality, badly damaged, and would not be considered acceptable for exhibition in any major museum. But to a small museum which had nothing similar, they were something, and consequently the destruction was a loss to someone. But it is also true that some important objects were exported and whether that was "bad" or "good" is a moral judgment that can vary according to the time and circumstances. I recall vividly the occasion when this truth was brought home to me. I was aboard the *S.S. Exolona* acting on the orders of President Roosevelt as a United States Marshall assigned to return Mr. Samuel Insull to the United States. Mr. Insull in conversation with me defended his actions, which the prosecutor claimed to be criminal, as being legal at the time when taken. He illustrated his point with this story, "Berry, you know, if a citizen were to walk down Fifth Avenue in New York last year with a fifth of whiskey and a twenty dollar gold piece in his pocket, he could have been arrested for having possession of the whiskey. Then, if he, as Rip van Winkle, took a long sleep, and on awakening walked down Fifth Avenue with the same fifth of whiskey and the same twenty dollar gold piece in his pocket, he could have been arrested for having the gold piece, for in the interval the possession of liquor had been made legal and the possession of gold by private individuals had been made illegal!" Perhaps, in final analysis, all that can be said on the subject is that each person makes his contribution which is judged according to the mood of the times.

Just as with the stories of Nasreddin Hoja anyone could have easily become fascinated with the old bronzes found in the Istanbul Bazaar, and collected, and studied, and written of them ad infinitum as I am tempted to do here. Once the interest was aroused in any such object, whether prehistoric figurines or Byzantine crosses, the material was available for the asking. But, except for the person who was born with collecting in his blood, perhaps the most considerate advice for the visitor to the Bedestan would be to paraphrase Whittemore's advice to the tourist who called on him in Istanbul forty years ago. "Visit," he said, "the museum of Greek and Roman antiquities, quickly determine the sex of the statues, and then leave at once."

Pectoral cross. Bronze. Byzantine. Fifth century A.D.

Plates for Chapter V

Page

41. *1.* Turkish door discs of the sixteenth to eighteenth centuries.   113
    2. Turkish door discs of the sixteenth to seventeenth centuries.
    3. Turkish door discs of the eighteenth to nineteenth centuries.

    Illustrative of the little bronze animals that were available in quantity in the Bedestan in the 1930s are those shown here:

42. *1.* A fifth-century B.C. bronze horse. Phrygian appendage from a bronze vessel. The head is turned slightly right, the right leg raised, the mane, neck muscles, and collar indicated by incisures.   114
    2. A fifth-century B.C. bronze deer. Achaemenidian appliqué for a belt or some other leather object. The deer is resting, but alert. Above its back is some conventionalized foliage, perhaps indicating a forest scene. The modeling is good and the preservation excellent. Appliqués such as this were used as ornaments on all manner of fashionable leather objects of the time.
    3. A third-century B.C. bronze tortoise. Graeco-Roman fibula or brooch. The scales of the carapace are well defined by incisings. Reproductions of reptiles of all kinds in metal, glass, or semi-precious stones were popular for personal ornaments for both men and women throughout the Roman world.
    4. A second or first century B.C. bronze dog. Hellenistic statuette, once mounted on a base or affixed as an appendage to a larger object such as a bronze vessel or mirror. The dog is standing, alert but not aggressive. It has a collar around the neck.
    5. A bronze bull. Hellenistic or, more likely, first-century B.C. Roman, of imposing mien. The head is alert, the tail twitching, the dewlap well defined. Among antiquities Roman bulls are common, but this is an especially fine specimen. Likely it was made as a decorative statuette for a home.
    6. A bronze swan. First to second century A.D. Roman lamp feature. The swan has both wings partly raised and is preening its feathers which are indicated by incisings. The finer examples of Roman bronze lamps had covers over the holes through which oil was poured. These covers often were decorated with human or animal figures.   115

43. *7.* A bronze owl. Second to third century A.D. Roman statuette on a base. The feathers are indicated by incisings. The object likely was made as a decorative household ornament. The owl, known in Greek times as Athena's bird, in antiquity, as today, is associated with wisdom.
    8. A bronze ewe with nursing lamb, on pedestal. Second to third century A.D. Roman decorative household statuette. From earliest Christian times lambs were associated with Christianity and, somewhat like the peace symbols of the Hippies of the early 1970s, indicated a non-violent revolution to the positions taken by the "Establishment" of the

day. Statuettes of lambs were common in Roman and Byzantine times but those with ewe and lamb were more rare.

9. A bronze Byzantine ornamental holder for ferrous metal blade to be used in striking against flint to create sparks and make a fire. A stylized bird rests just above each finger hole. Some empty spaces are filled with incised circles.

10. A bronze cock. An eleventh-century A.D. Byzantine, or perhaps Seljuk, finial ornament.

11. A bronze donkey head. Second-century handle of a Roman table knife. The practice of decorating knife handles with human or animal heads was very popular in Roman times, especially in Egypt. The donkey indicates a heritage of Greek influence when the donkey was associated with Dionysus, the often drunk spirit of wine, hence appropriate for table cutlery. This handle was found in Egypt but I have seen similar, and even better, pieces offered for sale in the Istanbul Bazaar.

12. A bronze ox. Fourth-century Byzantine votive offering of a type surviving from Roman times and adopted by the Christians. On the shoulder is a cross followed by an inscription that is undeciphered.

All of these minor bronze figures save the last are at the Museum of Art, at Indiana University. The door discs are at the Art Institute of Chicago.

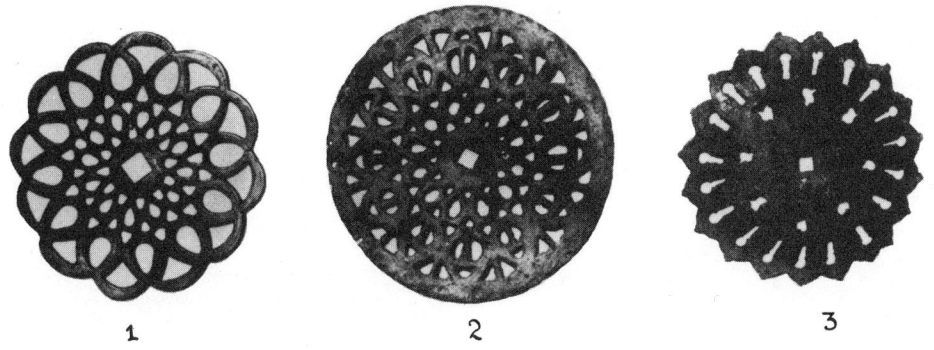

Fig. 1—Door Discs, Turkey XVI–XVIII Centuries

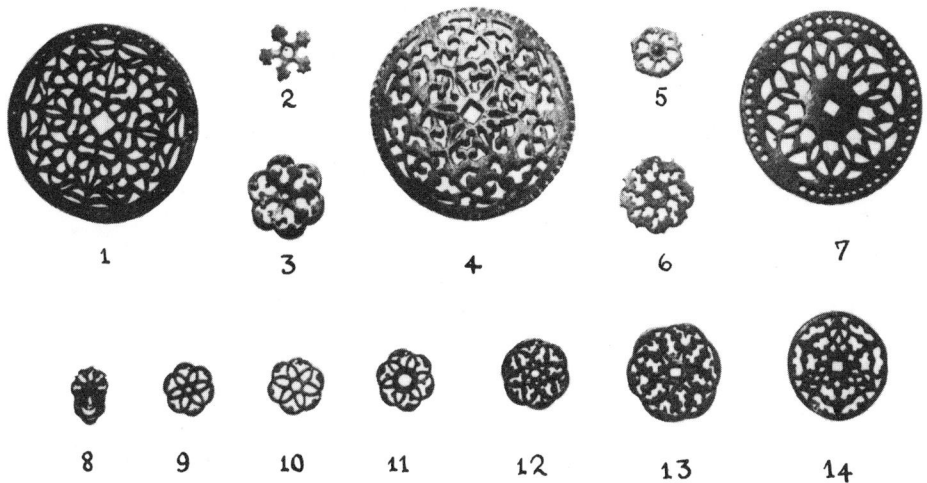

Fig. 2—Door Discs, Turkey XVI–XVII Centuries

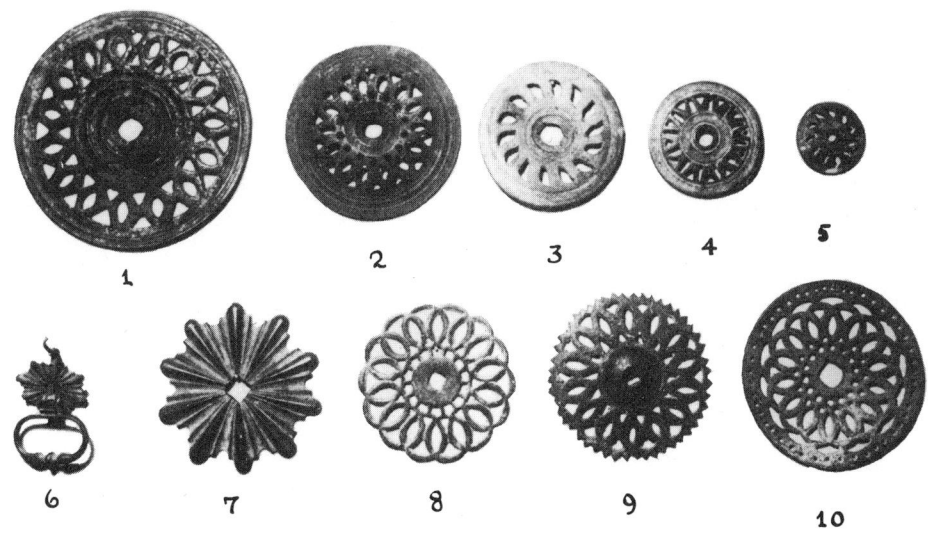

Fig. 3—Door Discs, Turkey XVIII–XIX Centuries

1
2

3
4

5
6

7

8

9

10

11

12

VI

Gem Stones and Jewelry

Engraved gems are a miniature art and as such they require minute contemplation to be enjoyed fully. They cannot be appreciated at a glance, yet the time spent studying the gems can be intensely rewarding. They are beautiful and they offer bits of evidence about people who lived long ago. The gems reflect in miniature the whole range of ancient art. They even provide evidence concerning long lost works of art. On ringstones we find perfectly preserved representations of contemporaneous life-size or larger-than-life statues, while in the great museums of the world the marbles in the round, in all but a very few instances, are only later copies of more ancient statues. Usually even these are mutilated, with arms, legs, or head missing. Indeed, the little gems merit our respectful attention.

Today, unlike coin collectors who are legion, antique gem collectors are relatively few in number. In the Istanbul Bazaar a tourist or a local person might buy an ancient ringstone for the purpose of making a signet ring but I know of only three collectors of ancient stones in Turkey: a local physician, a young Bazaar merchant who really likes stones and puts aside for his personal collection any superior piece that comes into his hands, and a Turkish businessman who in the course of his work travels extensively in Anatolia. The latter keeps careful records of his purchases and if one day he carries through his plans to publish a book about his collection it will be of great importance to every student of ancient gem stones for information about the finding place of a stone can be important. But the greatest amateur in Turkey that I have known was Osman Nuri Bey, who, as far as I know, had only one stone, but that stone he loved. Osman Bey was, at one time, an official of the Archaeological Museum, and then had a stall in the Bedestan which he relinquished when he grew older. Both of these events occurred before I knew him. Later he placed his stone in George Zacos' shop for sale. It remained there for many months but there was no buyer as the price asked was very high for the time. George returned the stone and a year later Osman Bey contacted me. He showed me his stone and told me this story.

In the first decade of the present century he visited Athens as a part of an official Turkish delegation and at a social event he was introduced to a lady who wore a gem stone as a brooch. He admired it and inquired about it but learned little beyond the fact that it had been found in Thessaly. But the stone had gotten into his blood so he sought out the lady later and told her that one of his great interests in life was antique engraved stones, and that he would gladly pay very well for her stone. She said that she liked her brooch and the stone was not for sale. Osman replied that he realized that would probably be the case but perhaps she might be willing to exchange the agate stone in the brooch for a diamond of equal size! The lady hesitated and so the matter was referred to her husband who, being a man of commerce, quickly accepted. Now, as Osman said, times had changed and he wished to sell his stone. The price was very high, even for a stone the size of a large rose diamond, and so I did not buy it. But the stone also "had gotten into my blood" and a few months later I sent the money from abroad to Robert Mandil with the request to buy the stone even if he had to increase the price, which happily he did not have to do!

Osman Bey sold the ringstone that he loved, but another great amateur of stones threw his away! This was Polycrates. The time was the sixth century before Christ. The story that comes down from

Osman Bey's gem stone. Nude warrior with chlamys over his shoulder, helmet on his head, gorgon-decorated shield on his arm, and carrying a spear. He is standing, facing left, at ease, in the center, in front of his horse, which, facing left, lowers its head as if to drink. Ground line. Lenticular. Carnelian, slightly convex on both sides. 27 mm long, 22 mm wide. Circa 510 B.C. Found in Thessaly.

Herodotus via Seltman is this: On the independent island of Samos there lived one Polycrates, the eldest son of Aiakes, a wealthy and highly respected nobleman of the island. Now at that time the people of Samos were in a high state of excitement as the expanding Persian Empire had recently engulfed the Kingdom of Lydia which lay just across a narrow strait from Samos. Polycrates took advantage of the popular mood and seized the administrative authority on the island, making himself the Tyrant. His strategy for preserving the independence of his homeland was to develop the Samian war fleet, and then to consolidate it with the fleets of other Aegean islands and ally himself with Amasis, Pharaoh of Egypt. He would thus weld together a great maritime power with which to check the Persian advances. And in all his efforts Polycrates was consistently successful.

Besides being an able ruler and the architect of a strategy for stopping the westward expansion of the mighty Persian Empire, Polycrates was also a patron of the arts. He commissioned Theodoros, a fellow Samian who was celebrated as an engraver of gems, to make a ring for him with the signet engraved on an emerald.

Now the Pharaoh Amasis, a good but superstitious man, being informed of the unbounded success of his ally, Polycrates, wrote to him saying that his success could be the cause of his final disaster as the gods were jealous. Amasis suggested that Polycrates propitiate the gods by choosing from his treasures whatever he held most valuable and then disposing of it so that it would never again be seen by men. Polycrates reflected upon the advice of his friend and decided that of all his possessions what he held most valuable was his signet ring. He put to sea in a vessel of fifty oars and when in deep water before the eyes of all men he cast his ring into the sea, then returned to his house and mourned his loss.

Polycrates' choice of his engraved emerald signet ring as his most valued possession provides the reason for including the story here, but the story also has its merit as a story and so, parenthetically, the end is also included for the sake of those who may not recall the final scene. It is this: Some days later a fisherman working his trade near Samos caught a splendid fish. He thought that such a fish deserved to be presented to the Tyrant Polycrates so he took his catch to the Palace rather than to the market. The Tyrant was pleased to accept the gift and when his cook opened the fish to prepare it for dinner he found the Tyrant's emerald signet ring in its stomach! Pharaoh Amasis, on being informed of these events, felt that man could not be protected from his own fate and wrote to Polycrates ending the alliance. Of course, Polycrates eventually lost his life at the hands of an agent of the Persian king!

In his admiration for his engraved ringstone, Polycrates was a typical Greek aristocrat. We know from many ancient authors that throughout the whole Greek world fine engraved stones were held in high regard as works of art. But it was in the later Roman world, particularly in the late Republican and

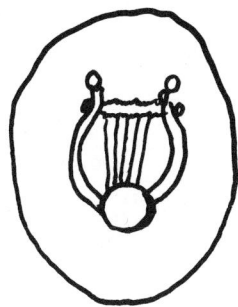

Polycrates' emerald ringstone is said to have been engraved with a lyre. This stone is an amethyst set in its original gold ring. 11 mm long, 9 mm wide. Roman art.

Imperial times after Rome had established her military position of power and authority and yet was enslaved by Greek cultural achievements, that engraved stones became generally popular. Rich and famous people collected and filled cabinets with them. Some, who were philanthropists, placed their collections in the sanctuaries of their favorite gods where they could be seen and enjoyed by many people. The less rich showed their wealth by the engraved stones they wore. By the time of the later Roman emperors, every free man aspired to have one or more engraved stones, usually with each set in a ring. Intense rivalry developed among collectors and the prices paid for fine stones rose exceedingly high.

After the break-up of the Roman Empire, fine stones continued to be engraved in Byzantine and other cultural centers. Some of these stones have come down to us but the records concerning them are few and incomplete. It was only with the Renaissance that the fashion for all classical things brought back into high favor finely engraved stones, both ancient and newly engraved ones inspired by the ancient. We know something, too, of the values placed on them. For example, Pope Paul II (1464-1471) offered to build at his own expense a badly needed bridge for the city of Toulouse in exchange for an ancient engraved stone, but his offer was refused. Popular interest in engraved stones continued until the early nineteenth century when, following the disclosure of considerable counterfeiting, it fell away sharply.

It is indeed fortunate today that private antique gem collectors are relatively few in number as the newly found material arriving on the market is very limited; in the antique market where there is a strong demand and a short supply, the forgers make their appearance. Moreover, in addition to the private collectors who are buying antique gems, there is a demand for them from those people who admire antique art in all its forms and enjoy owning one or several antique engraved stones. Then, too, the great museums in America and abroad, which have gem collections, some of them founded several generations ago, are always seeking to improve their collections. The competition is keen and there is always a thrill in acquiring a fine stone.

The oldest engraved gems were made as seals and were worn on strings around the neck or on the wrist, but in Greek and later times the sealstones usually were set in finger rings. Until the end of the Roman Republic, such a finger ring was normally the only ring worn. From then on, the wearing of finger rings, set with engraved stones, became increasingly fashionable, until in the late Roman Empire, both men and women wore rings on all fingers, and sometimes two or three to a finger.

Some stones cut in intaglio were also made to be worn as amulets, protecting the wearer, according to the strength of his belief, against all manner of calumny. Although generally apotropaic, such amulets were also often considered beneficent. Certain stones, engraved as amulets in Roman times, were supposed to possess in themselves magical qualities; the amethyst was thought to prevent drunkenness, some agates were said to be beneficial against the bites of scorpions, and the diamond was thought to be a cure for insanity.

And, particularly after the Hellenistic period, although intaglio ringstones and amulets continued to be made, many gems were created to be used as ornaments on jewelry, and for the decoration of gold and silver vessels, and even furniture.

The designs engraved on gems reflect the fashion of their day. The principal motif, until the late Roman period, was pictorial. The owner's name was sometimes included but as a subordinate part of the composition. The designs included reproductions of statues of deities, heroes, portraits, animals, and scenes from daily life. The earliest stones, Eastern, Minoan, and Mycenean, usually pictured some form of animal life as a main motif. The Greeks chose favorite deities, legendary heroes, or subjects from the animal kingdom for their signets. The Romans, while adopting Greek ideas and motifs, extended the list by including portraits, many subjects from daily life, animals, objects, and fantastic creatures. A portrait on a Roman stone might be of an admired Greek personality long dead, of a distinguished ancestor of the owner, of a living friend, or of the leader of some group of which the owner was an adherent. The early Christian and Byzantine gems emphasized religious motifs. In the Christian period we first find signet rings where the motif is exclusively the monogram of the owner, the early form being a block monogram and the later one a cruciform monogram. In looking at the designs on engraved gems it must be remembered that intaglios were usually made as sealstones and should be looked at from the impressions, the exceptions being generally amulets and late Roman intaglios obviously made for the decoration of vessels and furniture.

Our knowledge of the technique of engraving gems in ancient times is deduced largely from the stones themselves. All the stones shown here seem to have been made with the wheel technique although some of the work on certain Roman pieces was finished with a sharp cutting point, perhaps a diamond point. The engraving was done, as far as we know, without the use of a magnifying glass, with simple tools, a wheel or bow, several types of drills, a graver, and some cutting powder mixed with oil. The design was first sketched out and then the actual cutting was done with some very hard powdered stone mixed with oil and directed by a drill powered by a wheel or bow which was presumably operated by hand. Whether the stone was stationary and the drill mobile, or the stone mobile and the drill stationary is not definitely known, but there are adherents to each theory. After the engraving was completed the stone was usually highly polished. The work must have taken tremendous patience and skill.

The vast majority of ancient gems were not signed. Illustrated here are no ancient gems bearing names that can safely be attributed to the engraver. When there is a descriptive indication it refers to the owner, or the subject pictured. On those gems where engravers' signatures do occur, they are small and inconspicuously placed. It is a fact that, in the great museums having gem collections, ancient signatures occur on some gems of poor quality, while many of the finest ancient gems in the world are unsigned. Nevertheless, a signature adds something of interest to any gem and increases its value. Because of this, in the eighteenth and nineteenth centuries particularly, ancient gems were copied and signatures placed on the copies. Sometimes, too, signatures were added later to authentic gems to increase their value, but such forgeries do not remain undetected long.

It has been suggested by several scholars that the artists who made the engraved gems were sometimes the same artists who made the dies for the coins of the day. This seems to me to be both logical and likely, although in my own experience I have found no clear proof of the theory. But the fact remains that there is a close affinity between stones and coins. Of the two, engraved stones being individual, and bearing a personal signet, can be more appealing than the coins which are popular and bear a city or federal signet. Moreover, the fact that a stone is one of a kind has its special attraction. Being one of a kind does not mean that a magnificent statue by some great sculptor such as Phidias, Polyclitus, or Praxiteles, or a statue of a mighty deity, such as Athena or Apollo, or of a popular philosopher, such as Socrates, did not prove an inspiration for many artists who engraved gems. They did indeed. But, nevertheless, there is an individuality about each gem, since the owner chose the material, its size, color, and shape, and the artist developed the design according to his own individual feelings. The variation of designs within the same theme on similar stones can be both intriguing and delightful. This applies to all ancient gems, with, of course, the exception of cast glass paste. In the end it is really the immense variety of subjects engraved on the gems that challenges one's interest most deeply. They provide a source of study and satisfaction practically without end.

Ringstones, unlike coins, never come on the market in hoards. They are found one by one, often in old cemeteries. Country jewelers buy them from the finders and when they come to Istanbul they bring what they have assembled to the Bazaar. Frequently the stones are chipped or broken and this is usually because the present day finders have sought to pry the stones free from their settings. It must be remembered that most finger rings before the time of the Roman Empire were of bronze or iron and that these metals deteriorate when buried in the soil for long. Thus, the rings normally were found damaged or broken and the peasant-finder thinks that the value of the stone is enhanced by removing the stone from the damaged ring. While I have never seen a hoard of ringstones I did see in the Bazaar a section of a great hoard of ancient clay impressions of ringstones which was found in the Mersin area several years ago. They were Roman and not extraordinary in quality and may have been all that remains of a great file of records, such as wills, or of manuscripts in a library. I bought none, but advised the finder to take the entire hoard to the Archaeological Museum in Istanbul as it had research value.

Today a great many of the jewelers having shops in the Istanbul Grand Bazaar are from Mardin. Among the first of these to transfer to Istanbul were two men who had been partners in the jewelry business in Mardin. In the Bazaar these men were known as "The Partners" and they continued their partnership for many years in Istanbul. They were active, eager to learn, and, from my own experience, correct in their dealings. Before coming to Istanbul they manufactured in their shop in Mardin earrings,

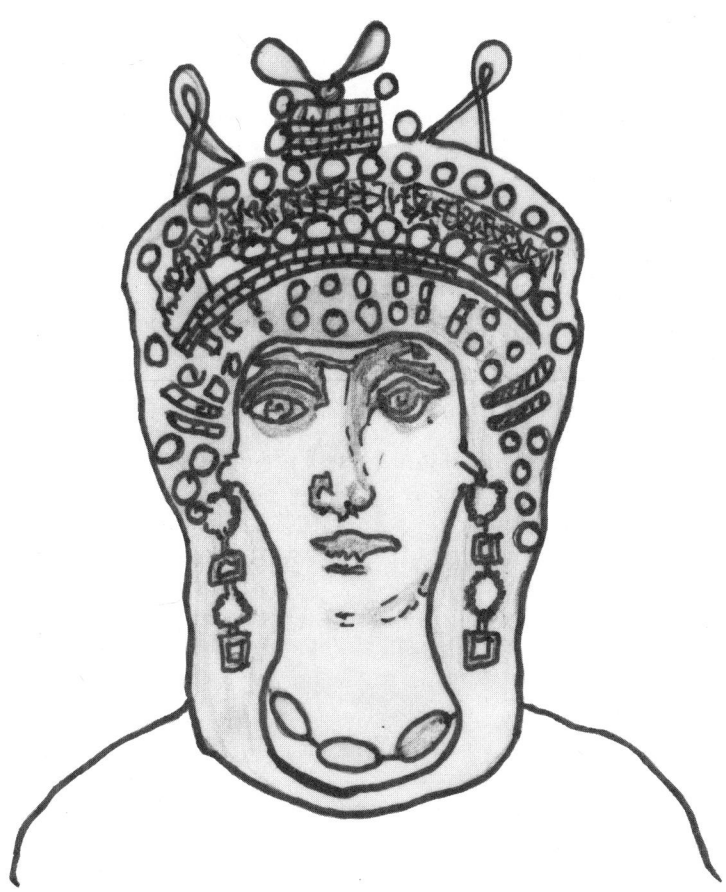

Mosaic portrait of the head of the Byzantine Empress Theodora, showing her jewelry. Detail from a mosaic in the Church of San Vitale, Ravenna, Italy, 547 A.D.

Gem Stones and Jewelry

bracelets, and other pieces of jewelry for the country trade, and traveled through Anatolia selling these articles to village merchants. On establishing themselves in Istanbul they had a large acquaintanceship among the country jewelers who, on coming to the city, sought them out. In fact just as Osman used to receive most of the itinerant clothing peddlers coming from Anatolia with their bales of towels and old clothes, so "The Partners" used to receive the village jewelers and the men who traveled about buying old silver and gold, which included watch cases, peasant jewelry, and occasionally archaeological objects. Often they arranged that these men show whatever they brought at the hour that I normally visited their shop. Then we would pour the contents of each valise into a pile in the middle of the floor and, sitting on low stools around it, separate the haul into piles for melting, for repairing, and for selling as it was. Sometimes I was joined in this operation by my friend Nicolas Karageorge and, with "The Partners" over glasses of tea, we had many pleasant times, punctuated occasionally by an argument or a flare of temper. As with most things in the Bazaar this was a cyclic affair, with a small beginning, several years of great activity, then a tapering off as the material began to move directly from Anatolia to Europe, and, finally, an end when my own interest decreased and "The Partners" terminated their partnership. There were two other shops which I visited that operated along the same lines, and three men whose business was exclusively smelting. These were also good friends. One day I was called to one of these shops for a first viewing of some merchandise from Anatolia. When I arrived I found that the material had been seen and picked over by many people, and I expressed my disgust. One of "The Partners," who was present, said to the shopkeeper that he should not have acted in this way and offered diluted material as Mr. Berry had been around almost as long as Nasreddin Hoja. I asked him to make himself clearer and he told this story: "One of his parishioners brought Nasreddin Hoja a gift of a hare. He was warmly thanked and invited to remain to dinner and partake of his gift. The next week the peasant returned without a gift but he was hospitably received. The following week several strangers arrived at the Hoja's house and asked to be entertained. 'Who are you?' asked Nasreddin. 'We,' they replied, 'are the neighbors of the man who brought you the hare.' 'Welcome,' said the Hoja as he set cups of water before them. 'Come, now, Hoja,' said the strangers, 'what is this water that you have set before us?' 'That is not water,' replied Nasreddin. 'That is the soup of the soup of the hare.' "

One of the antique dealers of the Bazaar complained to me that I was "opening the eyes" of "The Partners." I said that that was exactly what I hoped to do, as they had told me that they had melted four kilos of antique gold objects in Mardin to get the metal to make modern jewelry and I considered that this was a loss to civilization.

I wanted them, and everybody, to realize that by such actions they were destroying something of value to make something of less value, and when everybody understood this then mankind would be the richer. Certainly from Mr. Karageorge and me "The Partners" made their profit, and learned what we could tell them and thereby profited still more. But when we were available we had "first refusal" of the material received and, although at this writing I recall no great coup that I brought off, the impression remains of a long and pleasant association. Moreover, what was most important, the material was not destroyed.

For me the most interesting of all experiences would occur on those days when someone from the country would arrive with a few objects tied in a handkerchief, objects that had been found all together. These were "grave finds" which really came out when a farmer was working his land and his plow entered a tomb of an ancient cemetery. In these finds there was normally a handful of glass beads, that once had been a necklace, usually a pair of earrings, sometimes a finger ring and/or a bracelet. Commercially the lot was of very little value, and archaeologically it was of no value at all as it had come from an "uncontrolled dig," but to me it was interesting to see what was used together at any certain time. Of course, the interest was greatest when what was presented came from a single grave, for then there was no intrusion of objects from an earlier or a later period. Occasionally two or more beads would be stuck together by the action of some fluid and the earth, and once in a great while by vestiges of string, and this was always a happy occasion as it provided evidence of the arrangement of the beads on the original necklace. On those rare occasions when the necklace, fragmentary or intact, was of gold ornamented with pearls or stone or glass beads, that was a day for rejoicing and celebrating with a second

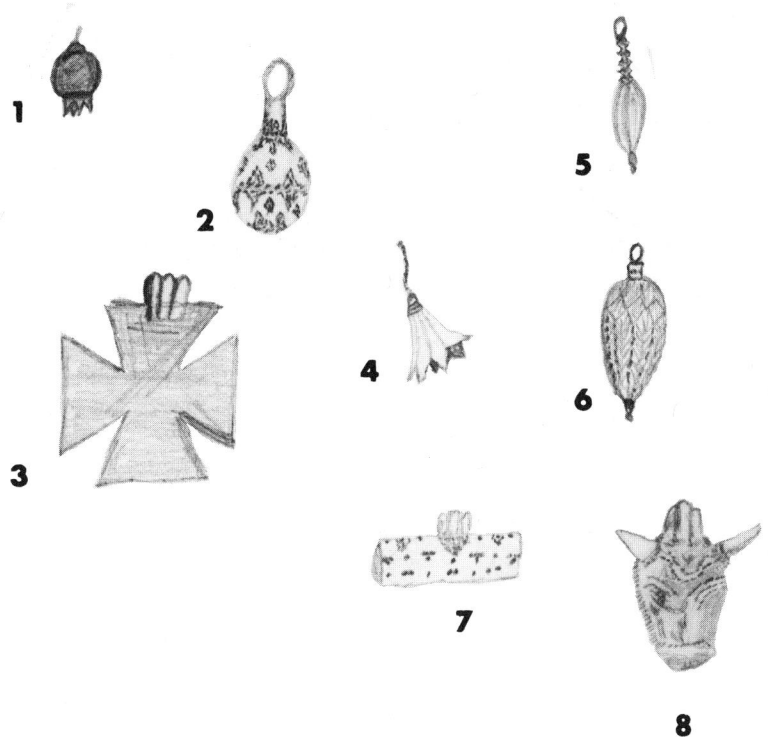

Gold pendants from ancient jewelry. 1, seventh century B.C. from Kammeros; 2, seventh to sixth century B.C. from Phoenicia; 3, seventh to sixth century B.C. from Phoenicia; 4, fourth century B.C. from Greece; 5, fourth century B.C. from Greece; 6, fourth to third century B.C., Hellenistic; 7, second century B.C., Roman; 8, seventh century B.C. from Rhodes.

glass of tea! Most of this jewelry shown at "The Partners" was of the Roman period and the jewelry was "of the people." The metal was usually gold. In the shop I could select from the peasants but I had to leave my selections until "The Partners" showed them at the Museum and secured clearance to sell. This was the responsibility of every licensed dealer. Usually the permission was quickly granted but on those occasions when it was not I did not mind particularly as I had had the pleasure of seeing the arriving merchandise, and there never were enough funds anyway to buy all that I wished to buy!

On several occasions I have used the phrase "of the people" and one rightly can ask: But, who were the people? In ancient Egypt they were those around the Pharaoh: the royal family, the ladies of the harem, the priests, and the military leaders. Similarly, in other ancient Near Eastern civilizations, as we are concerned with them here, the people, those that possessed gold jewelry, were the persons that were a part of the court at Alacahoyuk, at Mycenae, and at the palace cities of Crete. However, beginning in classical Greek times, with colonies being established by Greek cities in barbarian lands, with commerce increasing, and wealth diffused beyond the circle of political and religious leaders, the possession of jewelry was more widely spread. The people then included the colonial leaders, the rich merchants, and the successful naval and military captains. And, after the Asian conquest of Alexander the Great, with the distribution of booty to his loyal soldiers, the number of people who possessed jewelry was further expanded. Later, in the period of Roman domination, all freeborn men and women used jewelry as lavishly as their wealth permitted, some going so far as to wear a ring below each joint of each finger on both hands. Emperor Caligula, who loved display, appeared in public wearing jeweled rings, bracelets, pins, cloaks, and shoes, and even gave a necklace set with precious stones to his favorite horse! And the style the Emperor set was followed by lesser persons according to their wealth and inclination. In

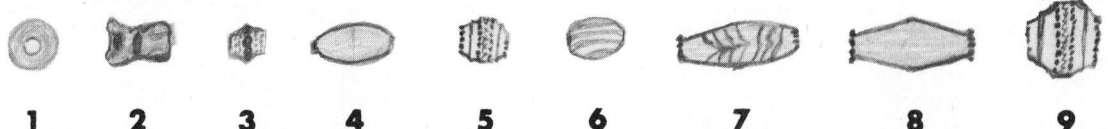

Gold beads from ancient jewelry. 1, from Cyprus, Mycenaean period; 2, from Ephesus, eighth century B.C.; 3, from Ephesus, eighth century B.C.; 4, from Ephesus, eighth century B.C.; 5, from Phoenicia, seventh to fifth century B.C.; 6, from Phoenicia, seventh to fifth century B.C.; 7, from Greece, third century B.C.; 8, from Syria, Roman, first to third century A.D.; 9, from Syria, Roman, third century A.D.

Byzantine times, too, the court set the example and the people, which by then included everyone who had the means, followed its example in the use of jewelry. For these later periods of antiquity, the Hellenistic, Graeco-Roman, Roman, and Byzantine, when jewelry was widely produced and popularly used, very similar examples of jewelry could surface in very different parts of the ancient world. Personally I had the experience of seeing objects unearthed near Antakya which were apparently identical to objects I had bought and know were recovered from the soil near Alexandria, Egypt. Both could be interchanged, almost without detection, with objects in the Naples Museum that were excavated at Pompeii. Such is evidence of the universality of styles at a given epoch in the ancient world.

In the Bazaar gold jewelry from the "high period," represented by the finds of Alacahoyuk, was exceedingly rare but stone beads that had been elements of necklaces and gold objects did show up from time to time. Also there occasionally appeared some items of jewelry from ancient Egypt and Mesopotamia, giving witness to the fact that there was trade and diplomatic exchange of gifts in remote times. Finely made Greek jewelry of classical times was rare but Hellenistic jewelry in fine examples was always to be seen, while the "bourgeois" Roman and Byzantine jewelry was so plentiful at times in the Bazaar that it found no immediate buyer. In addition to the gold, jewelry in silver and bronze appeared from every historical period. Usually the metal indicated the social class of the original owner, but it was the gold in ancient and modern times that caught the eye.

This was partly due to the fact that from Hellenistic times gold was more plentiful than in earlier periods. New sources had been discovered in Macedonia on Mount Pangaeus and were exploited by Philip II, the father of Alexander the Great. The latter in his victorious march across Asia captured vast quantities of gold as booty which was distributed to his soldiers. Moreover, in Hellenistic times the wearing of jewelry was stylish, and much was made and much has survived as gold does not corrode like silver or bronze.

Occasionally a gold or silver vessel or silver spoons from an historical period would appear on the market but the bulk of the ancient gold and silver that was for sale came in the form of jewelry. The most common objects were earrings, then came finger rings, followed by necklaces, bracelets, brooches, pins, and diadems. There were also mouth pieces and finger rings which were of very thin gold and made especially for interment with the bodies of deceased persons. This funeral jewelry, not being usable today and usually of poor quality, was often melted for the metal value.

Several excellent books have appeared recently on the subject of ancient jewelry and so it would be pointless here to go into a detailed discussion of the manufacturing techniques. It is sufficient to say that many, but not all, finger rings were solid cast in molds, then hammered. Other objects were hammered from sheet gold and ornamented with gold wire or chased or engraved, with colored stones or glass added. Thin plaques to be sewed on clothing were stamped. Chains made from gold wire were popular as necklaces. We find examples of these even in the tombs of the early Kings of Egypt. In the Classical and Hellenistic times wire was braided into a rope, or a flat strap, from which hung pendants in the form of arrowheads or amphorae. Other ropes without pendants, had a knot of Herakles as the centerpiece and a clasp formed by confronted heads of women, or heads of lions, bulls, antelopes, or other animals. Much of this jewelry is beautifully designed and made.

When discussing jewelry I was often asked, "What will you do with it after you get it?" Personally I have always enjoyed studying the jewelry as facets of ancient civilizations, and for the jewelry itself, and then giving it to museums where other people can see and enjoy it. At times I have displayed some pieces in vitrines in my home where they have elicited enthusiastic comments. I have found that ancient jewelry shows off best when displayed with glass objects of the same period as the iridescence on the glass complements the stones and glass on the jewelry to make a pleasant ensemble.

Intaglio stones as elements of jewelry have been discussed. Pearls and cameos in Roman times, and stone and glass beads in all times, were used extensively. At the same time that I mention glass beads I should mention the glass cosmetic jars and vials which, with the jewelry, formed an essential part of the toilet necessities used by the ladies of ancient times to make themselves more attractive. Dating this glass was always a problem. I recall showing a glass bead to Mr. R. A. Higgens, a keeper of Greek and Roman Antiquities in the British Museum and the author of an excellent book on ancient jewelry. I asked him his opinion of its date and manufacture. He shook his head and said, "These beads had a very long life." According to my experience he was absolutely right in two interpretations: Exactly similar beads were made in antiquity over a long period of time, sometimes as long as several hundred years; and such a bead once made, used, and lost, and then recovered after a thousand or more years of burial, could look like a new bead. The dating within a few decades of most ancient jewelry can best be accomplished by its association when found with other objects, particularly pottery and coins.

Stone funereal portrait of a Roman lady of Palmyra, Syria, wearing her jewelry, 161 A.D.

Plates for Chapter VI

Illustrated here are 27 enlarged impressions of gem stones selected for the beauty of the stones, the craftsmanship, and the variety of the designs. The actual size of the maximum carved surface is indicated in millimeters in the description of each stone. The stones are all intaglios, that is, cut in indentation. Until the time of Alexander the Great engraved stones were intaglios, and most of them were made to be used as signets to be impressed on wafers of wax attached to documents, or lumps of clay to seal doors, or cabinets, or jars of wine or oil, for in ancient times a personal seal had the same authority that a signature has today. They are from the collection of the Museum of Art of Indiana University. Any one of them could have emerged from the Istanbul Bazaar, but as I have no record before me I cannot be certain where each was bought. Buying a stone was for me a relatively rare occasion, and I thought at the time that I would always remember the details, so with them, unlike with coins, I made no record, and, of course, with the passing of years the details became blurred and eventually lapsed altogether from my mind! But as Merinsky would have said, "That, sir, may be an advantage!"

Page

44. *1.* Graeco-Persian. Wild boar running right as if pursued. Second half of the fifth century B.C. Scaraboid. Bluish chalcedony. Perforated, 23 mm long.   131
    2. Greek. A heron, with aigrette on its head, in profile to the left searching for food. Second half of the fifth-century B.C. Scaraboid. Chalcedony. Perforated, 27 mm long.
    3. Roman. Capricorn swimming to right. Carnelian. 17 mm long.
    4. Roman. Shrimp, head to right. Red jasper. 15 mm long.
    5. Roman. Two horses cavorting. The nearer one lying on its left side and pawing the air with its feet. Its neck is arched, its mane windblown and it tosses a broken bridle with its head. The legs of the further horse are hidden by the body of the nearer but it appears to be running left as the neck is arched and the mane windblown. Octagonal carnelian ringstone. 15 mm long.
    6. Roman. Two goats confronted, rising on hind legs. White onyx. 14 mm in diameter.
    7. Roman. Toad seen from above. Red jasper. 11 mm long.
    8. Graeco-Roman. A hunter standing on the left, facing right, wearing an animal skin as a cloak, and carrying his hunting stick on his left shoulder. Before him, a ram. On the right, a tree from which hangs a dead rabbit. Ground line. Emerald. 9 mm long.
    9. Roman. Mask, facing slightly to the right, of a bald and bearded man. Nicolo. 12 mm long.

45. *10.* Hellenistic Greek. Bust of Apollo in right profile. Beneath a laurel wreath his long   132
hair falls onto his shoulders, which are clad in a chlamys. Before him the upper part of a lyre. Carnelian. 15 mm long.

11. Classical Greek. Head of Athena Parthenos in right profile. She wears a crested Corinthian helmet and a drop-type earring. Reddish brown glass paste. 19 mm long.

12. Roman. Bust of Asklepios, right profile. In front, the suggestion of a staff with serpent entwined around it. Gray and black onyx. 13 mm long.

13. Hellenistic Greek. Bust of a young woman in profile to the right with narrow fillet across forehead and wavy hair falling loosely on her right shoulder, wearing chiton. Perhaps Medusa. Carnelian, chipped behind neck, at the bottom and before the face and neck. 21 mm long.

14. Roman. Head of Socrates in right profile, bald and bearded with characteristic short snub nose. Carnelian as originally set in an antique hollow gold finger ring. 15 mm long.

15. Hellenistic Greek. Portrait, in right profile, of a bearded Greek magistrate, philosopher, or intellectual; perhaps Hermachos or Epicurus. Carnelian. 20 mm long.

16. Hellenistic Greek. Bust of Nike in right profile, wearing chiton, hair worn in plaited curls with lock falling on neck. Over her shoulders the suggestion of wings. Carnelian. 11 mm long.

17. Graeco-Roman. Head of Herakles, wearing a lion's skin, right profile. Garnet. 18 mm long.

18. Roman. Bust of a mature woman, likely Faustina, in left profile. Her hair is bound with fillets with a flat knot of hair on the top of her head. She wears a chiton. Emerald. 16 mm long.

19. Roman. Zeus seated on right facing left, with a paten in his right hand, a staff in his left. Before him stands an eagle with head turned toward the god. On the left a winged Nike holds a garlanded wreath. Heliotrope. 14 mm long.

20. Hellenistic Greek. Priestess, wearing chiton, but with right breast and leg exposed, carrying an amphora and paten, making an offering before a small statue of Apollo which stands on a garlanded pillar. Carnelian. 25 mm long.

21. Roman. Zeus, the supreme god, god of the sky and weather, seated facing on a throne with a high back, holding in his right hand, Nike, goddess of victory, and a sceptre in his left hand. Near Zeus' right foot is an eagle and two grains of wheat. To the right of Zeus stands Hermes, Zeus' herald, nude and facing, holding a purse in his right hand, a kerykeion in his left hand. To the left of Zeus is a bust of Men, the Anatolian deity, in left profile, with a crescent moon behind his shoulders, and above his head a star. Grayish translucent agate. 15 mm long.

22. Roman. Eros, sleeping on the ground in the shade of a branch of a tree, on the left. His bow, quiver, and arrows are in a cloth tied to the branch. Ground line. Red jasper. 15 mm long.

23. Hellenistic Greek. From left to right, a tall column, Apollo wearing a himation and carrying his lyre in his left hand, then a branching tree, then a young satyr in the act of stringing up Marsyas by his hands with a rope thrown over the branch of a tree. Marsyas' feet are off the ground. Then, an altar, and finally a young man, wearing a Phrygian cap. He holds a knife above an altar. Ground line. Carnelian, chipped on upper edge. 18 mm long.

24. Roman. In the center, a low pillar upon which stands a sculpture representing the head of a bull. To the left, a celator, nude except for a chiton at his waist, seated on a rock, holding in his right hand a mallet which he uses in shaping a bull's head. Behind the bull's head, the draped figure of a genie. To the right, a seated male figure, wearing a himation and mantle, watching intently the progress of the work. Behind him, the completed body of the bull. On the ground, celator's tools. Ground line below celator and pillar. Sardonyx, slightly chipped around edges. 31 mm long.

Page

25. Roman. The bust of a female head, right, with the bust of male head forming the top of her head, the type known as a gryllos. Onyx. 13 mm long.

26. Byzantine. Cruciform monogram, which in translation reads, "The seal of Paul, Stratelates." Instead of being engraved on a stone, this is engraved directly on the bezel of a massive gold ring. 12 mm diameter.

27. Byzantine. Standing facing male figure, "The Good Shepherd," with head to the left. He wears a short tunic. On his shoulders he carries a sheep, facing left. At his feet, to the right, and to the left, stand lambs, looking up. In the left field, a Christogram. Ground line. Nicolo, chipped at top. 13 mm long.

The next three plates illustrate archeological jewelry from the Grand Bazaar in 1934. The objects shown are typical of what was available. Similar objects, and often far better specimens can be seen today in the Archeological Museum in Istanbul.

47. Early jewelry. Five bronze safety pins (with pins broken), Asia Minor, sixth century B.C. or earlier; four straight pins: a first-millennium bronze pin, a Roman bronze pin of a hand holding a ball, a Greek silver pin with a lynx head, a Greek bronze pin with a gold head; three gold Greek and Roman crescent pendants; a gold and onyx Roman pendant; a gold Roman terminal of a hand making the gesture of "fica"; two pairs of Greek gold earrings; and four gold finger rings, Greek and Roman.   134

48. Roman jewelry. Eleven types of Roman glass beads and two phallic glass pendants from necklaces; a necklace, fragmentary, of alternate garnet and gold spherical beads; a child's necklace of blue glass beads on a gold chain; a double loop in loop gold necklace, a pair of gold earrings each with a shell ornament and three pendants ending in carnelian beads, and gold pendant in the form of a shell. The last four items reportedly were found together and hence were known in the market as a "grave set."   135

49. Byzantine jewelry: a silver chain with pendant cross; two silver and two gold pendant crosses; two bronze pendant crosses; two pairs of gold earrings; a gold and agate finger ring and a silver finger ring with inscription; a gold chain necklace with pendant crescent and elaborate clasp; and a flattened gold chain necklace for a child.   136

Gem Stones and Jewelry

1

2

3

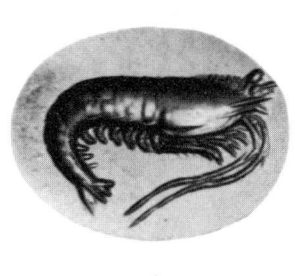

4

5

6

7

8

9

10

11
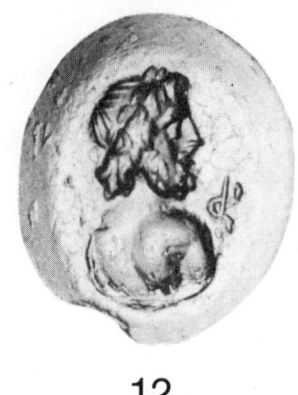
12

13

14

15

16

17

18

19

20

21

22

23

24

25

26

27

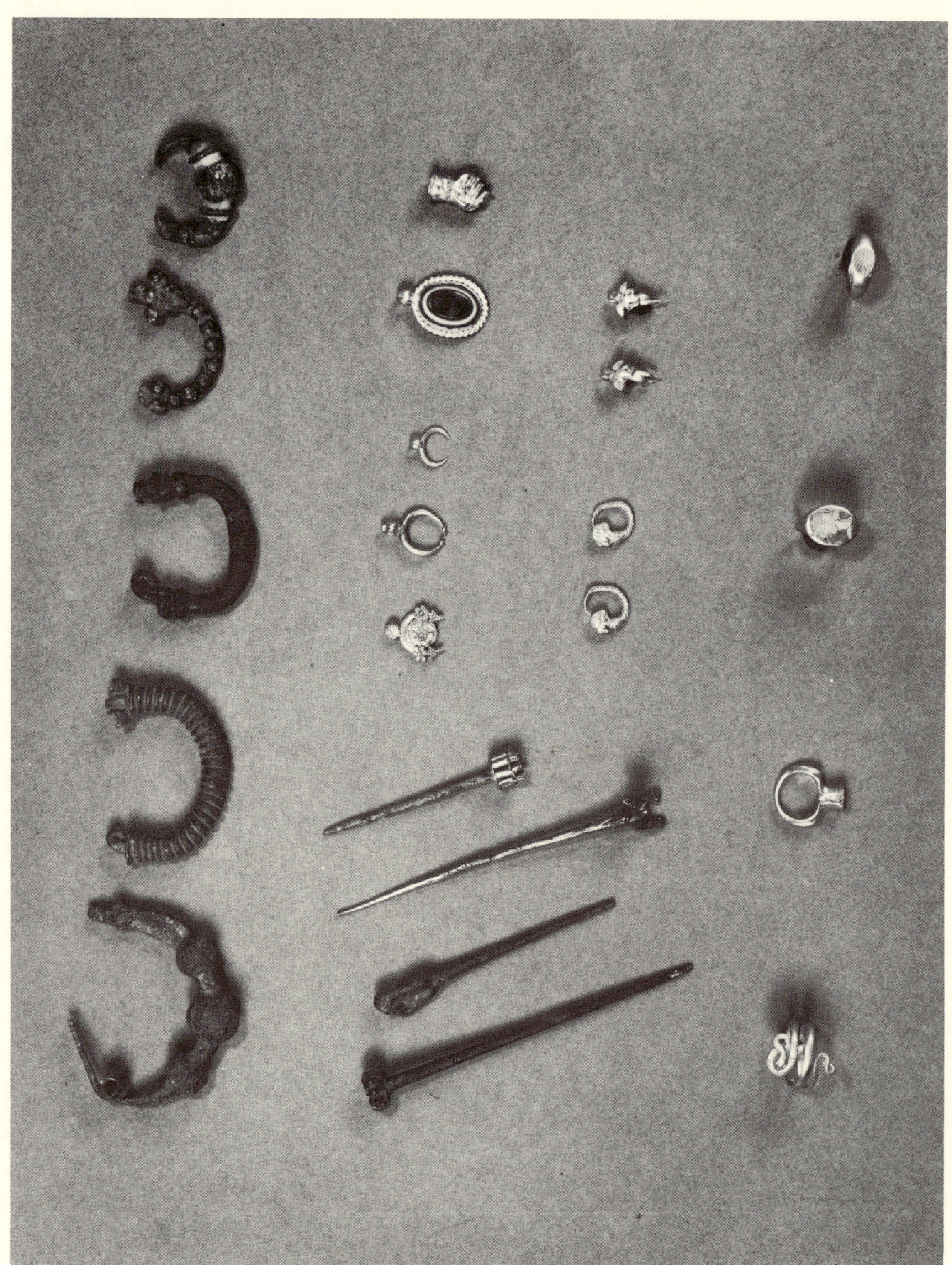

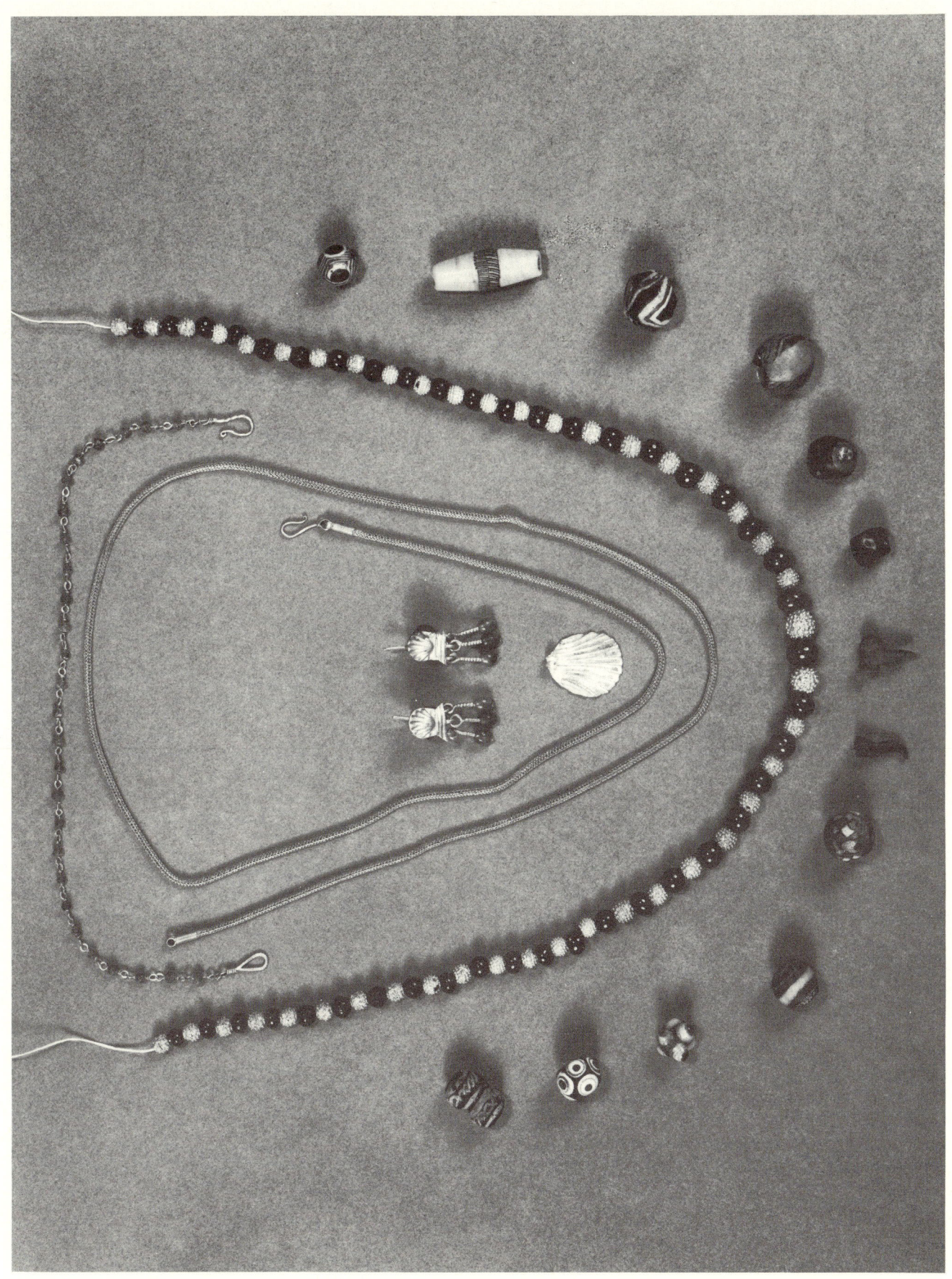

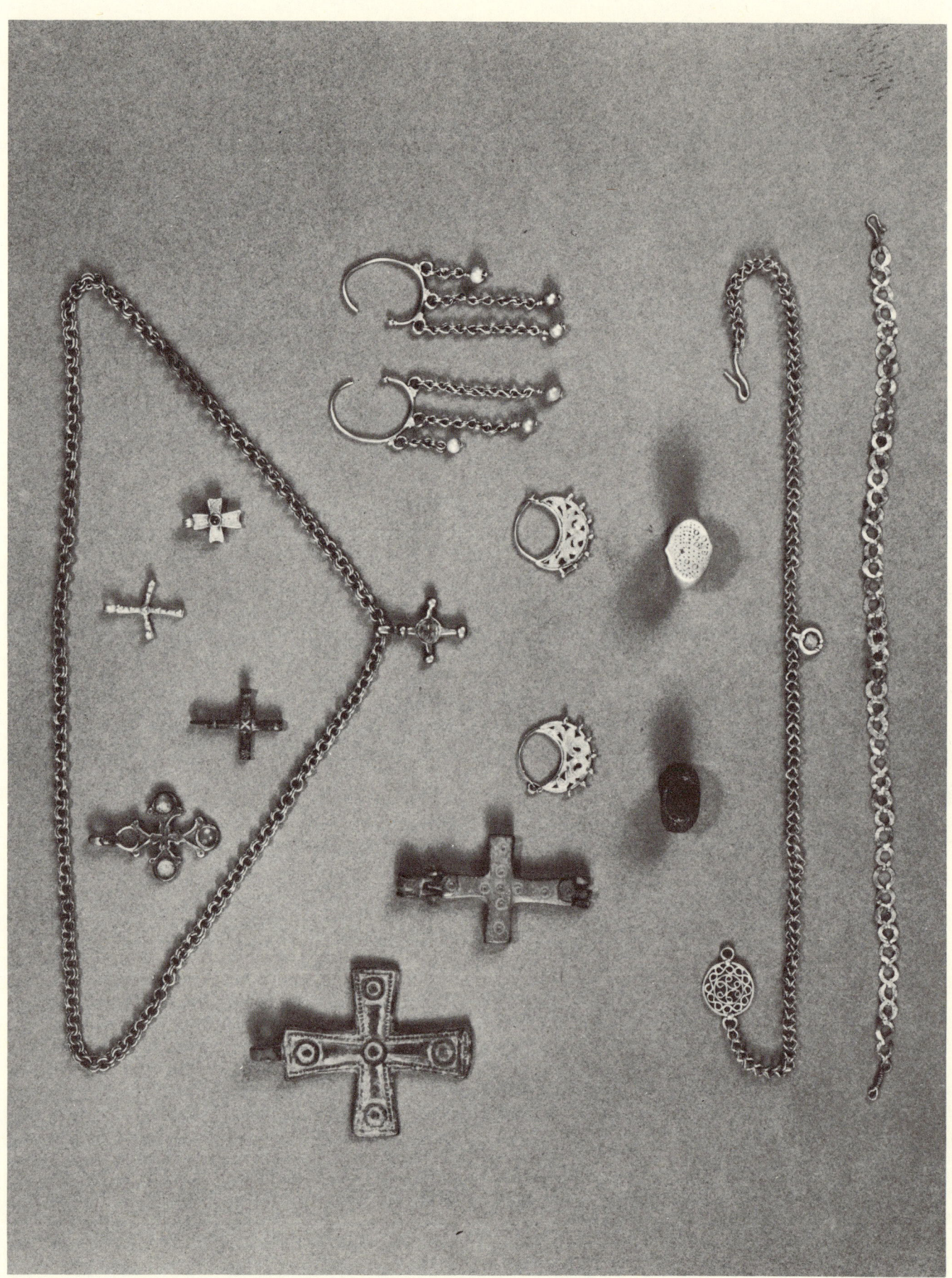

VII

Byzantine Solidi

For anyone who had a yen to collect Byzantine gold coins there was no more fortuitous set of circumstances than those existing in the Istanbul Bazaar from 1930 until about ten years ago. First of all, one had the immense advantage of knowing that he was living in the capital city of the Empire that for a thousand years had kept bright the beacon of civilization in Europe. Here history was made, Emperors came and went, and money was coined by them for use throughout the Empire. Istanbul, or Constantinople, as it was then called, throughout the life of the Byzantine Empire was the chief mint for coining money, and living in Istanbul, one was living at the source of supply.

Besides being present at the place of origin of the money of the Byzantine Empire one had the tremendous advantage of being present at a time when circumstances brought out of the ground an unprecedented number of treasures of Byzantine coins. They came out because of the surge of modernization which was set in motion by the reforms of Ataturk. The widening of old streets, and the cutting of new ones, the enlarging of public squares, the demolition of thousands of old houses and replacement of them by apartment buildings, the sinking of deep foundations for public structures, new canalizations, all those resulted in shifting acres of subsoil in the city, and from this came many coins. When earth was removed from excavations in Stambul it was the practice to haul it in great trucks and dump it in the sea on the Marmara shoreline between Kumkapi and Yedikule. Almost any day a person walking along this shore could see rows of trucks lined up to discharge their cargos. These mounds of earth remained intact until a storm came out of the south when the waves shifted and leveled them in a process of washing and rewashing until they were flattened and became an integral part of the beach. But the metal that the earth contained remained in place on top of the sand for the beachcombers to pick up. Looking back now it seems almost as though Providence was offering her treasures for free to anyone who wished them, but people were indifferent.

This of course was before Prime Minister Menderes built the great boulevard that follows the shoreline between the Byzantine sea walls and the sea, so that to get to the water's edge in those days one had to do a certain amount of scrambling. Some people did get there and they profited considerably. The south wind usually blew for three days running. After the third day the sea moderated and the harvest began. I recall that George Zacos told me that he always got to his shop early on the morning after a south wind in order to be present when the scavengers who tramped the coastline arrived at the Bazaar with their harvest.

One of the largest hoards of Byzantine gold, in my experience, came to light through the procedure of dumping unwanted earth in the sea. One trucker dumped his load and as the soil cascaded off the back of the truck a sharp-eyed worker caught the glint of gold. He pulled a gold coin from the soil and, when the driver went on his way, carefully sifted through the earth from the truck and found several more coins. These he brought to George Zacos who bought them and advised him to follow the truck to the place of excavation and perhaps there he might find more coins. This was done and a total of some thirty-five kilos of coins were recovered, about two thousand five hundred of them being confiscated by the Archaeological Museum. The coins were nomismata, the name used to describe slightly concave solidi, struck in the name of Andronicus II with Michael IX. In the Bazaar I was shown several bags of these coins, but, as my interest in Byzantine coins was much less than my interest in the Greek series, I did not have the patience to examine one by one the coins that added up to many kilos. Satiety, I have found, numbs one's sensibilities. However, I did quickly run through my fingers a kilo or two of coins separating what at first appeared to be the best struck, best preserved, specimens. These I examined more closely to select variations in style and monograms. In the end I bought a dozen or so pieces, other people bought more, and finally the great bulk of that part of the find that reached the Bazaar was melted down for gold as no one wanted it as coins. As far as I know this find, called the Cerrah Pasha hoard, was the largest find of the decade, but if one reduced it very substantially in scale, one can say it was a typical example of a hoard recovered twenty years ago, seen briefly by a few people, then melted down for the metal value.

In addition to being at the place where Byzantine coins were struck, and at the place where they were being recovered from the ground, the buyer of some years ago in Istanbul had other advantages. First, there was very little competition on the market. In the Bazaar I knew of only one person who was working seriously on building a collection of Byzantine solidi. In the city I knew of two people interested in seeing and buying Byzantine gold coins, but each of these was occupied full-time with other activities and so he only bought when the opportunity came to him. Then, finally, the local authorities were not particularly interested in the Byzantine series. They never passed an opportunity to add Byzantine coins to the Museum's trays but their enthusiasm was in other lines.

Today the collector asks why did the dealers not put away coins and hold them for an advance in price. The answer is very simple. In the first place, no coin dealer in the Bazaar thirty years ago had capital in excess of his normal current needs. Secondly, who would believe that the price would rise? After all, there was always a supply in excess of the demand. Why would this not continue to be so? New finds were always arriving which would satisfy the collectors, thus what was not sold of the old finds must be melted down and converted into bullion, which furnished the funds to buy the next lot that would come on the market. So, for the Bazaar merchants, the cycle developed: buy, sell, melt, buy, sell, etc. Of course this referred primarily to gold. Byzantine silver coins came in such small numbers as to be negligible, and copper coins, as coins, interested no local person at the time.

While my thoughts at the moment are on the present I think that it will be interesting to contrast the situation in the Bazaar thirty or more years ago with the situation today. As I have recounted elsewhere there really were only two dealers in archaeological objects in the Bazaar when I went there in 1928, and when these two retired there were four. By 1970 it seemed that every shopkeeper was an "antikaji." If he did not have objects displayed in his show window he would have them under the counter. Checking my impressions on the subject recently, I asked every shopkeeper on one street in the Bedestan who had no antiques on display, if he had antiques. The answer in all but one case was "Yes, please come in." And the person who said that he had none replied, "Why did you not come yesterday? A merchant from Germany bought everything I had." In former times the Istanbul merchants would call colleagues in Athens or Rome to come to Istanbul and buy their merchandise when they had bought a hoard of coins or some attractive object. Now many merchants travel to Europe at least once a year to view the market, and others send material to Europe with their compatriots who are working there.

In Western Germany alone there are half a million workers from Turkey, and there are tens of thousands more employed in other European countries. These people are generally well-liked as they are good workers. They are good citizens, too, who send home their earnings and bring back with them radios, refrigerators, television sets, and automobiles to increase the material wealth of their homeland. Many workers carry with them for sale in Europe artifacts found by their relatives on the land they cultivate. They sell these directly or hand them to a fellow citizen with more experience in selling to Europeans. Munich is the great center of this trade. I know of several merchants established in Switzerland and France who go to Munich regularly to buy antiques from Turkey, just as residents of Beyoglu in former times would visit the Stambul Bazaars to buy antiques. The trade is brisk, in fact so brisk that a Bazaar friend recently said to me with a wry smile, "The Istanbul Bazaar for antiques has been relocated in Munich." Several natives of Turkey, former merchants of the Bazaar, have established themselves in business in Europe and are respected and successful. At first thought this fact comes as a surprise but when one reflects a moment it is no more strange than for Mr. Mandil some seventy years ago to come from New York to Turkey, establish himself in the rug business, and become known as the "King of Carpets."

If I were pressed to state how I came to be interested in collecting Byzantine solidi I believe that I would attribute it to two circumstances. First, Mr. Whittemore had given me a book to read on the subject of Justinian and Theodora, and I was quite taken with the lady. Secondly, Mr. Alexander Veglery, on retiring from his work as an engineer for a large American company in Turkey, came to George's shop to work with George in the preparation of a treatise on Byzantine lead seals. Alexander, a Greek of Phanarite extraction, was a graduate of Robert College and descended from a long line of distinguished ancestors who had served the Ottoman Empire as Viziers, Foreign Ministers, provincial governors, and Princes of Samos. He was intensely interested in all things Byzantine, and a ready source of much useful information, with excellent English, Greek, and Turkish at his command. As I visited George's shop almost daily I was exposed to, and ultimately succumbed to, the subtle pressure from Alexander to join the very small group of collectors of Byzantine coins.

Justinian, the nephew and co-Emperor with Justin, according to Whittemore's book and confirmed by historical texts, was a cold, selfish, ungrateful misanthrope of a man who, at 35 years of age, announced to a scandalized world that he had married a circus performer from the demi-monde of Constantinople. That the lady was, but she was a great deal more. She was beautiful, talented, generous, loyal, courageous, and devoted to her husband. To her Justinian ultimately owed his throne, his life, and largely his place in history. In the course of the rebellion in 532 the Palace area was isolated and besieged by the rebels. At one time the mobs from the streets were hammering at the very land gates of the Palace itself, and, with only a few defenders within, the situation looked hopeless. The Emperor and his ministers cowered within the Palace and talked of flight by sea. Theodora addressed them, "Escape is very easy, my Emperor. You have but to go aboard a ship and sail away. Nor need you want, for you have gold in plenty. But I tell you that when you have deserted your post as Emperor you will taste the very bitterness of death; and I your wife will not fly. I will not live to see the day when my purple robes are torn from me and I am Queen and Mistress no more. Let us remain at our post and fight until the last.

Follis of Justinian I.

If we die we meet our fate as becomes us, for the Empire is a glorious winding sheet!" The speech inspired the courage for a last desperate sortie. It was successful. The troops of the Emperor triumphed over the rebels. Justinian and Theodora kept their throne, she until her death from cancer sixteen years later, with Justinian surviving her for another seventeen years. In the Bazaar the coins of Justinian were plentiful but there are no gold coins struck with the portrait of and in the name of Theodora, however she left her imprint on whatever her husband did and history calls him "Justinian the Great."

After finishing Whittemore's book, I thought, if this is a lady of Byzantium then give me more. I asked Veglery to recommend other books and he made a short list which I bought, and read, and they became a part of me. Then when he urged me anew to start to collect Byzantine coins, I said, "O.K., but the ladies first." And so my first Byzantine purchase was a solidus, the gold unit of currency weighing 4.40 grams, of the wife of the first Byzantine Emperor. Her name was Eudoxia and she was the wife of the Emperor Arcadius. Arcadius inherited the throne at the age of eighteen. During his youth he was completely dominated by a scheming minister named Rufinus, who, to solidify his own position, arranged to betroth his own daughter to the Emperor. Arcadius went along with the plan, but during a temporary absence of Rufinus a member of the Emperor's household introduced him secretly to a beautiful Frankish girl called Eudoxia. On Rufinus' return he announced the forthcoming public betrothal of his daughter and the Emperor. For the day fixed the city was decorated and people lined the streets to see the brilliant procession leave the Palace headed by the Emperor and bearing his gifts of clothing and jewelry to the future Empress. To the shock of Rufinus and the surprise of the people the procession made an unscheduled stop at a house along the way; the Emperor's confidant entered and brought out Eudoxia who the Emperor acknowledged as his future bride! The failure of Rufinus' intrigue left him discredited and he was murdered; the person who engineered his deception and fall from favor was himself soon thereafter exiled and killed, while Eudoxia emerged as the sole victor and the power behind the throne until her own death. The coins of Eudoxia are relatively rare, as indeed are the gold coins of all the Byzantine Empresses, but there was a choice on the market and I chose from the best preserved as the foundation piece of my Byzantine collection.

Arcadius and Eudoxia had four daughters and one son, the future Emperor Theodosius. The daughters publicly declared themselves in the service of God and the eldest of them, Pulcheria, assumed charge of the education of their young brother who became an orphan and an Emperor at the age of fourteen. When she considered her brother ready, Pulcheria chose for his wife a beautiful and talented girl called Athenais. This lady was the daughter of a rich citizen of Athens who in dying left all his property to his sons stating that his daughter's natural endowments were sufficient inheritance. She disagreed, contested the will, and brought her case to Constantinople where she came to the notice of Pulcheria. I do not know whether she won her lawsuit but she certainly did win Pulcheria's confidence, was baptized in the state religion as Aelia Eudocia, and married the Emperor. She lived for years apparently happily with the Emperor and in excellent relationship with her powerful sister-in-law until a court intrigue caused her downfall and exile to Jerusalem. She passed her last years in the Holy Land occupied with pious works. Her coins are very similar to those of her mother-in-law with a slightly different spelling of the name, the letter "c" being used in place of an "x."

Upon Eudocia's banishment Pulcheria again dominated the court, and at the Emperor's death she inherited the throne. At that time she was in her fifties and as the people liked to have an Emperor she chose as her consort a professional soldier, named Marcian, who was then in his sixties, offering him her hand and her throne on condition that he respect her virginity as, it will be recalled, she had as a young woman offered herself to the service of God. Marcian accepted the condition and together they ruled a peaceful and happy Empire until Pulcheria died four years later to be followed in another two years by Marcian's own death.

After Marcian's death the next Emperor was Leo who was elevated to the throne by General Aspar, the Commander of the Imperial Guards. Leo's wife was named Verina and they had a daughter called Ariadne. These characters became involved in a complicated plot the like of which in our times is often described by the adjective, Byzantine. The plot unfolded in this way. The newly created Emperor betrothed his daughter Ariadne to the son of General Aspar as an acknowledgment of the debt to Aspar and as a form of recompense for his services. But as Aspar was very unpopular with the masses at that time the people revolted on hearing the news. This was in line with Leo's secret desires and, at his command, Aspar was treacherously murdered by one of his officers named Zeno, who shortly thereafter was betrothed and married to Ariadne as *his* recompense! The Emperor Leo, having no son, named as his heir the son of Zeno and Ariadne, also named Leo after his grandfather. Zeno saw to it that the little boy lived only a few months after his installation as Emperor, and later, Zeno himself, according to one account, was caused to be buried alive by Ariadne in order that she might be free to offer her hand to Anastasius, a guard's officer in his sixties! The man accepted, became a good Emperor, and, like the other members of his adopted family, died a violent death, being struck by lightning. No historian that I have followed has suggested that this was arranged by Ariadne! The solidi of Verina and of Ariadne are exceedingly rare and, although I know of examples having been sold in the Bazaar, I was not around at the time. I did, however, buy a treminus, a coin a third of the weight of a solidus, of Verina and one of Ariadne which I was happy to add to my growing collection of Byzantine Empresses.

And now we have to pass nearly three hundred years of Byzantine history before we find another solidus bearing the head of an Empress. This next lady to enter my gallery was Irene. She was the wife of Leo IV and the mother of Constantine VI who was crowned at the age of five and inherited the throne at the age of ten. Irene was an Athenian, beautiful but strong willed, domineering and scheming, whose ambition was to be the sole ruler. She prepared for this role by denying her son the education that would help him to reign. When Constantine became of age he demanded his rights and Irene responded by seizing his supporters and throwing the young sovereign himself into prison. The army rose in Constantine's support and Irene, realizing her mistake, immediately released Constantine. She was lightly punished, then forgiven, and Constantine took the field at the head of his armies to fight the enemies of the Empire, leaving his mother in charge in the capital. Irene then openly schemed to discredit her son, finally going so far as to send emissaries to kill him. He managed to escape these men only to be seized by some of his supposedly loyal followers, who had been blackmailed by Irene. He was bound and taken to the very room of his birth in the Palace where, at the bidding of his mother, his eyes were cut out with the rough knife of a common soldier. As a blind man cannot be Emperor, Irene, dignified by the Church with the title "The Most Pious," was left in sole possession of the throne. She had obtained her life ambition but she enjoyed it for less than five years as her Treasurer, Nicephorus, revolted, seized the throne, and exiled the Empress to the Island of Lesbos where for the remaining months of her life she made her living by spinning. As a poor blind monk, Constantine lingered on for many years. As Empress, Irene struck three types of solidi, each of which is shown here.

The Emperor Theophilus, whose wife was another Theodora, whose son became Michael III, and whose daughter was named Tecla, was a person whom I would like to have known. His character had many facets. He was passionately fond of gems, embroidery, and all forms of art, especially those made of gold and silver. He visited the Bazaar frequently, inspecting the wares and setting a control on the prices, especially those of the people's food. He was a competent military commander and good civil administrator. He and his wife held widely different views on important issues but theirs was an affectionate union that lasted until the Emperor's death. Normally Byzantine Emperors were aloof persons but Theophilus inaugurated a weekly drive from the Palace to the Church and on this drive he was accessible to any subject who had a grievance. On one such drive a man complained that the Emperor was riding his horse! The Emperor investigated, found the allegation to be true, and then offered the man the return of the horse or a generous payment in gold. By such acts the Emperor endeared himself to the people, and long after his death he was held in affectionate remembrance. On his death he set up a regency for his infant son but his wife, Theodora, took in charge the young Emperor, and soon had the government as well under her control. Her portrait appears on one issue of the coins of her son with his portrait, and on another issue with her son and her daughter, Tecla.

And now we come to one of the strangest periods in the whole of Byzantine history during which two royal Princesses played active roles in the lives of five Emperors. At the start of this period the great Basil II had just died, leaving his brother Constantine, a playboy well into his sixties, as his successor. Constantine had no son but three daughters, Eudocia, who after a dreadful seige with smallpox had hidden herself in a convent, and Zoe and Theodora, both middle-aged and unmarried. The succession required a suitable husband for at least one of the Princesses. For this Constantine's eye fell on an elderly noble, Romanus Aygerus, but as he was married, a trick had to be used. A company of soldiers called at Romanus' house, told him that he had angered the Emperor, and that his wife, to save herself, should immediately take the vows of a nun, and that he himself should go with the soldiers to the place of his execution. The wife took the vows at once and then Romanus was led before the Emperor, and told to marry one of the Princesses! As he was then unmarried he could not refuse and Zoe became his wife. Constantine died three days later and Romanus became the sole Emperor. Zoe soon became suspicious of her sister and had her confined to a convent. Romanus conveniently died, by assassination, and the same evening Zoe married a servant, who now as Zoe's consort, mounted the throne as Michael IV. The handsome Michael turned out to be a hopeless epileptic and Zoe's infatuation faded. However, as the Imperial couple had no children they were constrained by custom to adopt an heir, and this was done in the person of Michael's nephew, the Emperor Michael dying shortly thereafter. The new Emperor, called Michael V, shared the throne briefly with Zoe. However, the young man was soon instigated by an uncle to depose the venerable lady and have her consecrated a nun. The populace, angered by this action, rose against the Emperor and demanded the return of Zoe. Within twenty-four hours Zoe was back on the throne! The mob also demanded the return of Theodora from her convent, and the young Emperor Michael with his ill-advising uncle, fearing for their own lives, sought sanctuary in a monastery. The two Empresses were formally reconciled and sat side by side on the throne while in the streets the mob howled for the blood of Michael and his uncle. Both men were promptly blinded by order of the Empresses. The people then clamored for an Emperor and so, after a couple of months, Zoe took a new husband who mounted the throne as Constantine IX. This gentleman had been one of her admirers thirty years before and consented to return to her as her husband only if he could bring his mistress along! And so it was arranged. Theodora then returned to the convent, and Zoe soon after died. Constantine's health deteriorated and the seventy-year-old Theodora was once again brought back to the Palace from the convent. She capably took over the management of the affairs of state for the last few months of Constantine's life, then reigned alone for nearly two years until her own death, nominating an elderly soldier as her successor. The gold solidus of Zoe and Theodora was exceedingly rare until a hoard of some twenty pieces was found near Akcakoca and turned up in the Istanbul Bazaar to the delight of every collector.

As the final entry in my gallery of Byzantine Empresses I chose Eudocia Makrembolitissa if for no other reason than because of the fine Byzantine manner in which she successfully resolved her problem. The dying Emperor Constantine X exacted from his wife, Eudocia, a promise not to remarry, sworn to in the presence of the great of the land, and confirmed by a statement signed and deposited with the Patriarch. Eudocia, as Regent for her minor sons, applied herself to governing and did well, but the people desired an adult Emperor. She, a woman of fifty, who for some time had had her eye on a handsome noble of thirty, was willing. But her signed and sworn statement was inviolate. She appealed to the Patriarch but he was unmoved until Eudocia had a courtier hint to him that she had secretly selected the Patriarch's own brother as her new husband and Emperor. Then the Patriarch began to see events in a different light: the oath was given under duress, the need of the Empire for an adult Emperor was urgent; yes, the oath was really invalid having been extracted from the Empress by a jealous and dying husband; and so the Patriarch stated to the Senate, and the same day returned to the Empress the signed document. The very night that she got back her oath not to remarry she secretly married the handsome young noble, Romanus Diogenes, to the chagrin of the disillusioned old Patriarch!

There were other Byzantine Empresses whose portraits were in my gallery, such as Eudocia, the wife of Basil I; Marie, a provincial Princess who married the Emperor Michael VII and was famous for her extraordinary beauty; and Anna of Savoy who as the wife of Andronicus III and the mother of John V showed herself to be a capable sovereign; indeed, all remarkable women, but I must now exercise discipline to avoid straying too far afield from the purpose of this book, which is neither a history nor a numismatic text but one which relates primarily to the objects once available in the Grand Bazaar, with some indication of their antecedents.

In beginning my collection I started out to get a gold coin of each Empress and when I had exhausted all possibilities I reset my sights to get an example of each gold Byzantine issue by an Emperor or Empress. I did not succeed in this, lacking some twenty odd pieces when my interest faded, and I transferred my modest collection to the American Numismatic Society where it would be available to students. But, while I was active, the stocks of the Bazaar merchants, some other sources, and newly found treasures provided many opportunities. One of the sources that might surprise the Western collector was the dentists of Anatolian rural communities. It seems that when a peasant came into unexpected wealth he very often would elect to spend some of his money, as a status symbol, on new gold teeth. If he had found an ancient gold coin or two he would go to the nearest dentist and exchange the coins for new teeth. Sometimes the dentist would work the coins into teeth, but more often he used dental gold to make the teeth and saved the old coins to sell to some collector. From several country dentists came rare and beautiful Byzantine coins. During my active years, in addition to the immense Cerrah Pasha hoard of coins of Andronikos and the small hoard of solidi of Zoe and Theodora from Akcakoca that I have mentioned, there were many interesting discoveries. On the market these were known as finds, or as sections of finds, one rarely knew the full truth. Among these were some thousands of coins of Constantine II and Constantine IV from the Mardin area; a still larger find of solidi of Justin II from the Izmir region; twelve hundred or more coins of Basil I and his family from Camlica; five hundred of Arcadius, Theodosius, and the early Emperors from Stambul; two hundred pieces in mint condition of Justinian II, Tiberius III, Filipus Barbanes, Anastasius II, and Theodosius III from Adapazar; literally thousands of coins of the reigns of Heraclius and Focas from the Aegean area; hundreds of Alexis I and his successors from the Iznik country; a large quantity of Anastasius from Antalya; about one hundred splendid Theophilus from Bolu; and a great lot of Justin and Justinian from near Bilecik. My purchases from these great treasures were very modest as one coin of a series satisfied my desires. But my interest in seeing the coins, and hearing the stories about their discovery, and studying the history of the periods that the coins represented, was almost boundless, or so it must have seemed to the Bazaar merchants!

Plates for Chapter VII

Illustrations for this chapter are a series of Byzantine solidi. They are, of course, only a selection of the Byzantine coinage chosen for their interest and variety of types in well-preserved specimens. The descriptions of the solidi are simplified and the inscriptions omitted entirely as inscriptions on Byzantine coins, containing Greek, Latin, and local letterforms, certainly would be bewildering to the average reader, as indeed they are to some advanced students! Anyone wishing to go more deeply into the subject should consult one of the recent works on Byzantine numismatics such as the Catalogue of the Dumbarton Oaks and Whittemore Collections. The casual reader should be aware of the frequent recurrence of some names such as Eudocia, Theodora, and Zoe which were popular throughout Byzantine history, thereby creating at times identity problems. The coins are in the trays of the American Numismatic Society of New York. The photographs were taken by the Society's photographers in New York ten or more years ago.

EMPRESSES

Page

50. 1. Eudoxia, wife of Arcadius. 151
         Obverse: Bust of Empress to the right.
         Reverse: Victory seated right writing a Christogram on a shield.
     2. Eudocia, wife of Theodosius II.
         Bust of Empress to the right.
         Rome seated to the left.
     3. Pulcheria, wife of Marcian.
         Bust of Empress to the right.
         Victory to the left holding a long cross.
     4. Bust of Empress to the right.
         Victory to the left holding a long cross. Star in the field.
     5. Bust of Empress to the right.
         Victory seated right writing Christogram on a shield.
     6. Constantine VI with his mother Irene.
         Bust of Constantine VI, beardless, facing.
         Bust of Irene, facing, wearing crown with four projecting ornaments.
     7. Bust of Irene, facing, wearing crown with cross and two projecting ornaments.
         Same bust.
     8. On left, bust of Constantine VI, beardless, facing, and on right, bust of Irene wearing crown with four projecting ornaments.
         Three figures seated, namely Leo III, Constantine V, and Leo IV.

9. Michael III with his mother Theodora and eldest sister Tecla.
    Bust of Theodora, facing, wearing crown with cross and two projecting ornaments.
    Bust of child Michael on the left and taller half-length figure of Tecla on right.
10. On left, bust of Michael, beardless, facing, and on the right that of Theodora.
    Bust of Christ, facing.
11. Basil I with Eudocia and Constantine.
    Bust of Basil, bearded, facing.
    Bust of Constantine, beardless, on the left and bust of Eudocia on the right, both facing.
12. Constantine VII with Zoe, his mother.
    Bust of Constantine VII, beardless, facing, and bust of Zoe on the right.
    Christ seated, facing.
13. Zoe and Theodora, joint Empresses.
    Busts of the two Empresses, facing, holding a labarum.
    Virgin orans with a medallion on breast.
14. Theodora, Empress.
    Theodora, standing, facing, on the left with the Virgin on her right, they are holding a labarum.
    Christ, facing, standing on a footstool.
15. Bust of Theodora, facing.
    Bust of Christ, facing.
16. Eudocia, Makrembolitissa, Regent for her sons Michael VIII and Constantine.
    In the center Eudocia, standing, facing, on a footstool; on the left Michael and on the right Constantine.
    Christ seated on throne with back.
17. Romanus IV with Eudocia and her three sons.
    In the center Christ, standing on a footstool, with right hand crowning Romanus and with left hand crowning Eudocia.
    Michael VII in the center with Constantine on the left and Andronicus on the right.
18. Romanus IV with Eudocia.
    On the left, bust of Romanus IV, bearded, facing, and on the right, bust of Eudocia. They hold between them a globus surmounted by a tall cross.
    Bust of the Virgin, facing, holding a medallion of the infant Christ.
19. Michael VII and Maria his wife.
    On the left a bust of Michael VII, bearded, facing, and on the right a bust of Maria, facing, and holding between them a long cross ornamented with an X.
    Bust of the Virgin, facing, holding a medallion of the infant Christ.
20. Andronicus III with Anna of Savoy and John V.
    Andronicus III, bearded, kneeling, on the left, blessed by the Virgin standing right.
    Anna, standing, facing, on the left with John V on the right.

EMPERORS

51. 21. Arcadius.   152
    Profile bust of Arcadius to the right.
    Rome seated holding sceptre and globe.
22. Facing bust of Arcadius.
    Rome seated holding a spear and a Victory.

23. Theodosius II.
    Bust of Theodosius, facing.
    Emperor, standing.
24. Bust of Theodosius, facing.
    Theodosius seated with Valentinian III at his side.
25. Leo I.
    Bust of Leo, facing.
    Victory holding a long cross.
26. Zeno.
    Bust of Zeno, facing.
    Victory holding a long cross.
27. Anastasius.
    Bust of Anastasius, facing.
    Victory holding a long cross.
28. Justinian I.
    Bust of Justinian, facing.
    Victory, standing, facing, holding a long cross and globus.
29. Tiberius II.
    Bust of Tiberius, facing.
    Cross potent on four steps.
30. Maurice Tiberius.
    Emperor seated, facing.
    Victory, standing, facing, holding long cross terminating in a Christogram.
31. Focas.
    Bust of Focas facing.
    Victory, standing, facing, holding a long cross.
32. Heraclius.
    Bust of Heraclius, facing, bearded, wearing a crown.
    Cross potent on three steps.
33. Heraclius with his son Constantine.
    Bust of Heraclius on the left and Heraclius Constantine on the right.
    Cross potent on three steps.
34. Heraclius with Heraclius Constantine and Heraclonas.
    The three Augusti, standing, facing.
    Cross potent on three steps. Monogram in left field.
35. Constantine III, commonly called Constans II, son of Heraclius Constantine.
    Bust of the Emperor, facing, and wearing a crown.
    Cross potent on three steps.
36. Constans II with his son Constantine IV.
    Bust of Constans II with long beard and a smaller bust of Constantine IV, beardless, each wearing a crown.
    Cross potent on three steps.
37. Justinian II, first reign, son of Constantine IV.
    Bust of the Emperor, facing, and wearing a crown.
    Cross potent on three steps.
38. The Emperor, standing, with long cross on two steps in right hand (now often called the reverse).
    Bust of Christ, facing, with cross behind head.

39. Bust of Emperor, facing, and wearing crown, with long cross on two steps held in right hand and globus inscribed PAX in left hand.
    Bust of Christ, facing, with cross behind head; hair arranged in curls and beard short.
40. Leontius.
    Portrait bust of the Emperor holding mappa in uplifted right hand and globus in left hand.
    Cross potent on three steps.

52. 41. Tiberius III Apsimarus. 153
    Bust of Emperor facing wearing crown and cuirass and holding a shield and spear.
    Cross potent on three steps.
42. Justinian II, second reign.
    The beardless bust of the youthful Tiberius appears beside the bearded bust of his father, together holding a long cross.
    Bust of Christ facing with cross behind head, hair arranged in curls and with a short beard.
43. Filepicus, Bardanes.
    Bust of Emperor facing holding in right hand a globus and in the left hand an eagle-headed sceptre.
    Cross potent on three steps.
44. Anastasius II, Artemius.
    Bust of the Emperor facing carrying a globus in right hand and mappa in the left.
    Cross potent on three steps.
45. Theodosius III of Adramytium.
    Bust of the Emperor facing carrying a globus in right hand and mappa in the left.
    Cross potent on three steps.
46. Leo V, the Armenian.
    Bust of Leo V, bearded, facing, holding cross potent in right hand.
    Bust of Leo, facing, bearded, and holding globus in right hand.
47. Theophilus.
    Bust of Theophilus, bearded, facing.
    Patriarchal cross on two steps.
48. Alexander.
    Alexander, bearded, standing facing, on the left crowned by St. Alexander, bearded and bareheaded on the right.
    Christ seated facing.
49. Constantine VII alone.
    Bust of the Emperor, bearded, facing.
    Bust of Christ facing.
50. Romanus I with Constantine VII and Christopher.
    Romanus standing, bearded, on the left crowned by Christ standing on the right.
    Bust of Constantine VII, bearded, on the left and bust of Christopher bearded, on the right holding a patriarchal cross.
51. Basil II and Constantine VIII.
    Bust of Basil II, bearded, facing, on the left and of Constantine VIII, beardless, on the right, holding between them a patriarchal cross.
    Bust of Christ.

52. Constantine VIII alone.
   Bust of Constantine VIII, bearded and facing holding labarum.
   Bust of Christ, facing.
53. Michael IV, the Paphlagonian.
   Bust of Michael IV, bearded, facing, holding labarum and globus. Above Manus Dei.
   Bust of Christ facing.
54. Michael V, Kalaphates.
   On left Michael V, bearded, standing, facing and on the right the Virgin crowning him.
   Bust of Christ facing.
55. Michael VI, Stratioticus.
   Michael VI, bearded, standing facing on a footstool.
   Bust of the Virgin, orans.
56. Manuel I, Comnenus.
   Manuel I standing, facing, crowned by Manus Dei, and holding in his right hand a labarum and in his left a globus.
   Bust of Christ.
57. Andronicus I.
   Andronicus I with forked beard standing left, crowned by Christ, right.
   Virgin, seated, holding a medallion of Christ.
58. Issac II, Angelus.
   Issac II, bearded, standing facing on the left with St. Michael on the right. They hold between them a sheathed sword. Above Manus Dei.
   The Virgin seated on a throne with back, holding the infant Christ.
59. Michael VIII, Paleologus.
   On the left Michael VIII, bearded, kneeling, supported by St. Michael and crowned by Christ, seated on the right.
   The Virgin seated on a throne holding the infant Christ.
60. Andronicus II with his son Michael IX.
   Christ standing facing between Andronicus II kneeling on the left and Michael IX kneeling on the right.
   View on the walls of Constantinople with the Virgin orans in midst.

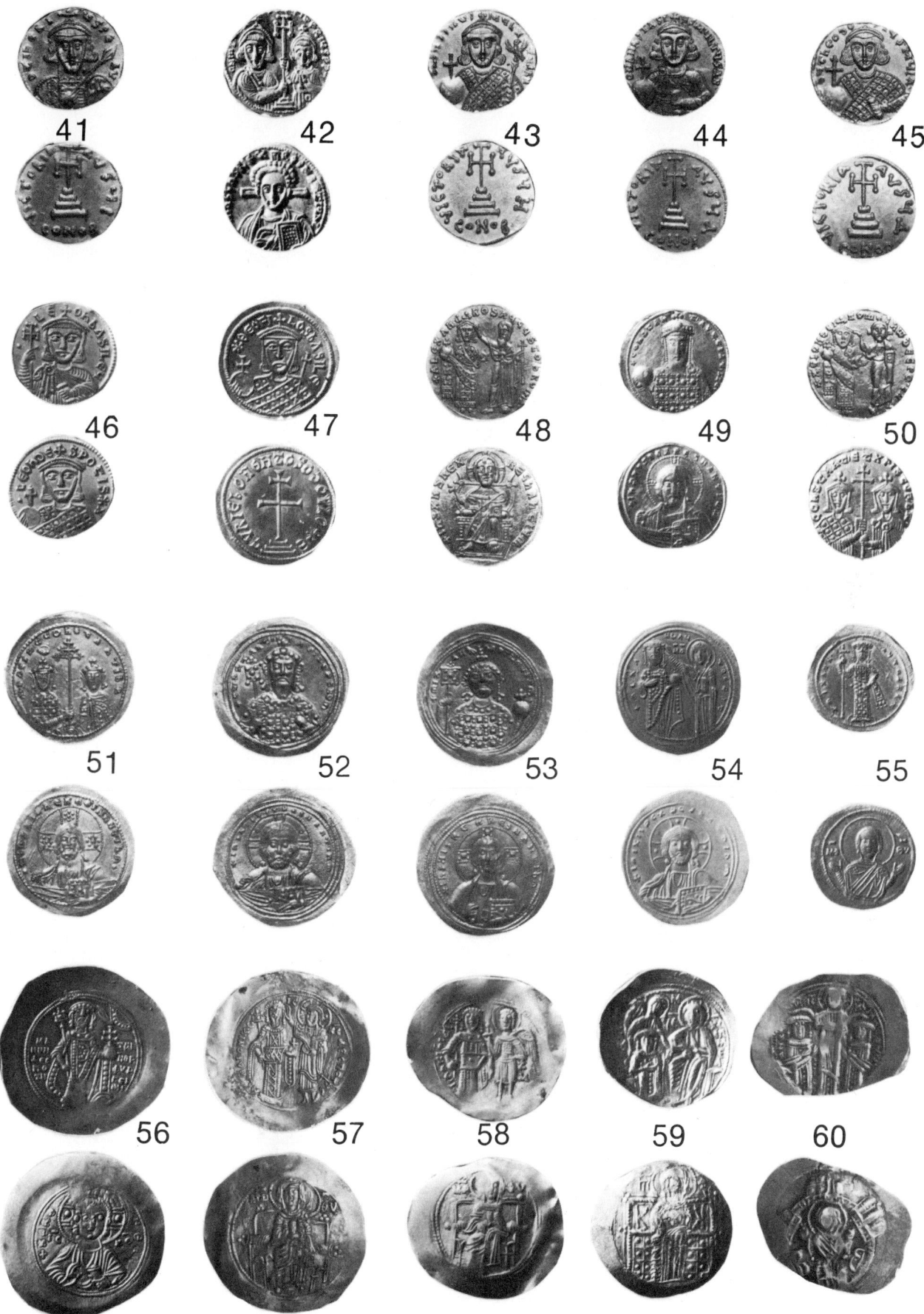

VIII

Ancient Greek Coins

Coins were invented in southwestern Turkey in a land called Lydia. The earliest coins were of pale gold stamped on the obverse side with an animal head and on the reverse with an incuse punch mark. They were probably first made for the purpose of paying mercenary soldiers in the employ of a king—certainly, at a much later date, we know that the first coinage of Carthage, made during the invasion of Sicily, was made to pay soldiers. Whatever the reason for the origin of the first coins they seemed to have found a ready acceptance locally as a medium of exchange and the first issue was followed soon thereafter by local coinages produced throughout the ancient world by kings and city-states. I saw some of these ancient coins in the Istanbul Bazaar in 1928 but they did not trigger my interest because at the time I was deeply concerned with the collection and study of certain old textiles. In fact so deeply was I engrossed with these that, although I was among the first to see one of the most spectacular hoards of ancient gold coins ever to be found, at the time I regarded the event as nothing more than an agreeable surprise met in the course of a pleasant Saturday excursion into the country!

One mild February Saturday when one felt spring in the air Vice Consul William Cramp and I decided that it was the day to make the long tour on foot around the island of Prinkipo, the largest of the Princes' islands which is located in the Marmara Sea about an hour by ferryboat from Istanbul. As we were finishing our tramp, approaching the village from the south, we met a little Greek boy who was crying. Cramp asked him what was the matter and he said, "They refuse to give me my part." We were moved by his tears and some apparent injustice done to him, so with his guidance we went to a nearby uncultivated field where two men were in earnest discussion. In those days workmen were inclined to be respectful to foreigners and so, when we indicated that we had come at the request of the boy, they told us their story. They were laborers working in the garden of a village landowner and had come to this empty field to get buckets of earth for the garden. In their digging they had come on a mass of large gold coins, which they had divided between them. The boy was simply a curious bystander, until the coins were found, and then he sought to become a participant, which they refused. The men showed us the coins, and asked if we would care to buy them at ten liras (about five dollars) each, but as neither of us had any interest in old coins we thanked them and went on our way.

On Monday morning I told Consul Charles Allen of the experience and said that I would like to return to Prinkipo and buy a coin or two as a souvenir of a very interesting day. He recommended against it, and I followed his advice, as he said that the find was treasure trove and the property of the state, and furthermore, as the treasure was of gold, the state would certainly claim its rights. On Wednesday the newspapers reported the find, and on the following Saturday, when I was visiting the Archaeological Museum, I called on the Assistant Director, Aziz Bey, who on other occasions had been kind and helpful, and told him my story. He was amused, and then added seriously that the purchase of old coins in the Bazaar from licensed dealers was quite alright, but that Mr. Allen was correct in advising me against buying from peasants as the Prinkipo find was an exceedingly important hoard of rare and beautiful coins which must be kept intact for scholars to study. Although six years were to pass before I bought my first ancient coin, the experience made quite an impression on me, and influenced me not to buy directly from the finders of virgin hoards.

The Istanbul Bazaar being what it was, one soon heard all manner of stories about the Prinkipo hoard and what happened to it. One story frequently told was that the hoard was sent to Ankara by night

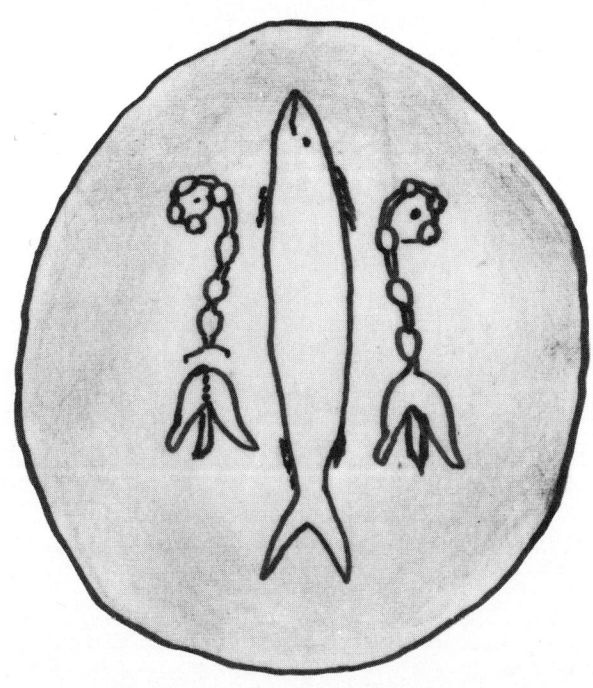

Electron stater of Cyzicus of the sixth century B.C.

express train in the custody of three civilian officers. Certain Bazaar merchants arranged to be passengers on the train, and these, like characters in a mystery novel, entertained the three officers at dinner where large amounts of alcohol were consumed. After dinner the officers in the warmth of the new friendship offered to show the coins, and on that occasion a number of coins were slyly removed from the hoard and an equal number of less valuable ancient gold coins substituted in order to keep the count correct. The story is false, but it proved useful to some merchants who had a stock of ancient gold coins and because of it, could pass off their merchandise to eager purchasers as a part of the Prinkipo hoard. It is true, on the other hand, that at least one person, Mr. Vladimir Elagin, was able to purchase a small number of coins from the finders before the police started to reassemble the parts of the hoard. To his credit it can be said that he showed his holdings to Professor Regling when he came to Istanbul at the invitation of the Turkish Government in 1930 to record the hoard scientifically. As all the Elagin pieces were duplicates or triplicates of coins in the Museum no objection was made to his continued possession of them. Much later Mr. Elagin was to sell me three of his Cyzicus staters from this hoard.

My second nudge toward becoming a coin collector, if you call seeing the Prinkipo hoard in situ a first nudge, came one afternoon in the autumn of 1935 when I was chatting with Mr. Theodore Zumbulakis of Athens in his shop. While we were talking of old textiles a farmer came in and offered Mr. Zumbulakis several large silver coins of Alexander the Great which the man said he had found while plowing his land. Mr. Zumbulakis bought them, showed and explained them to me, and remarked that now that I was living in Greece I should buy an ancient Greek coin or two. I did not buy, but the next time I saw some ancient Greek coins I really looked at them, and it was not long before Mr. Zumbulakis sold me a Greek coin—a tetradrachm of Alexander the Great similar to the ones he had bought from the farmer. Although I did not realize it at the time, this purchase marked my start as a coin collector, and when I returned to work in Istanbul, and started to visit the Bazaar again Greek coins replaced textiles as my principal interest.

Tetradrachm of Alexander III (336-323 B.C.).

Alexander III, or "the Great" as history called him, as soon as he had consolidated his position at home, started to realize his father's dream of crossing the Hellespont and conquering Asia. In doing this he was forced to import vast quantities of coins from his Macedonian mints, and later to establish mints in Asia Minor to produce coins. These were used, lost, and sometimes buried as treasure in his time. In our time some of these coins appeared in the Istanbul Bazaar, frequently as single pieces and occasionally as large hoards. Alexander's silver money, the tetradrachm, the drachm, and occasional larger and smaller pieces, showed in profile the head of young Heracles in a lion's skin on the obverse, and Zeus seated on a throne holding an eagle and resting on a sceptre, with the name of Alexander, on the reverse. While every tetradrachm is essentially like every other one, to the collector, every one is different, as even two coins from the same dies have a different aspect caused by the strike. In choosing coins for my collection my first concern was authenticity, and after that came style, condition of preservation, symbols, and mint marks.

Several weeks after I had bought my Alexander tetradrachm, Mr. Zumbulakis showed me a tetradrachm struck by Philip, Alexander's father. He told me how Philip's horse had won a race at the Olympic games, and that Philip, proud of his victory, had placed the image of his winning horse on the reverse of his silver coinage. I liked the story, and was pleased with the thought of having a coin of Philip of Macedon, so I bought the piece. I thought at the time that the die-sinker had never seen a racehorse, for his horse on the coin resembled one of those heavy draft animals which, at the time that I bought the coin, was used to pull beer barrel wagons. Nonetheless, it was certainly a mighty horse, and a mighty horse was appropriate for a memorable victory.

Philip's tetradrachms show on the obverse the laureate head of Zeus in profile. The reverses of some coins show a horse with a naked boy jockey bearing a palm. Other coins on the reverse show a bearded Macedonian horseman, wearing kausia and chlamys, with right arm raised. All reverses carry the name of Philip. Philip's silver coins turned up in the Istanbul Bazaar much less frequently than did Alexander's but they were seen, and sometimes they were of excellent style.

Philip, having gained possession of Mt. Pangaeus about 356 B.C., started to work its rich gold mines. The output was enormous, and the price of gold fell in relation to silver from 12 to 1 to 10 to 1. He used most of his mined gold in his coinage which proved very popular during his lifetime, and long after his death his coin types were reproduced by the barbarian tribes living in the hinterland. His gold coins were known as "Philippi." On the obverse is a profile head of Apollo, laureate and normally with short hair. On the reverse is the name of Philip and a biga, usually with the symbol of the mint of origin. The coins of Philip are usually very beautiful, in fact I think a fine stater ranks with the finest gold coins ever produced. The Prinkipo hoard contained some splendid Philip staters of unusual style and great beauty. Both Philip and Alexander staters were available in quantity in two shops in the Istanbul Bazaar in the 1930s.

Gold stater of Philip II (359-336 B.C.).

Having bought a coin of Alexander the Great and one of his father, Philip II, I thought it would be pleasant to hunt for some coins of their predecessors and successors. In time all these came out and the first was a tetradrachm of Alexander I, the first king of Macedonia. His reign of nearly forty-five years opened the coastal towns of Macedonia and Thrace to commerce. About 480 B.C., he conquered the neighboring Bisaltae tribes, the owners of rich silver mines. From one mine alone it is said that Alexander obtained a talent (about 58 pounds) of silver a day, striking his first regal coins from this silver. The earliest coins were crude, but coins in fine style soon followed. On the obverse, Alexander's coins show a horseman wearing kausia and chlamys and armed with two spears, riding right. Beneath the horse is the letter *A*. The reverse shows the forepart of a goat in an incuse square. Some coins of Alexander I, found in Thrace, found their way to the Istanbul Bazaar.

In the days before any of the antique dealers of the Bazaar had become competent numismatists I bought many coins from the bullion merchants whose only business was the buying and selling of precious metals. Generally they had no interest whatsoever in what you did with what they sold you. For them to receive a few percent above the normal selling price, in exchange for the privilege of choosing from the metal objects that they were preparing to smelt, was an unexpected bonus. But in buying from the gold and silversmiths the picture changed. They wanted to know why you wanted some coins and not others, and what you intended to do with what you bought. They were full of questions and curiosity, and parents of envy and jealousy, to the point where with some of them the really important question was not how much they profited from you but how much they feared that they lost by not knowing as much as you knew. But you had to buy where the material appeared and you had to act in buying according to your best judgment, and sometimes this proved to be very bad!

I recall an experience of an acquaintance, who was really a sly fellow, but on the surface was always pleasant and agreeable to the suppliers, and in a gesture of friendliness sometimes even paid more generously than they expected for a lot of coins. One day he called on a silversmith who had just received from Anatolia a consignment of old silver that included at least a kilo of archaic Greek silver coins in excellent preservation—a prize of a lifetime to a numismatist. My friend, seeking to dissimulate his enthusiasm, said that he thought that he could make something of the silver and would take the lot, paying handsomely for it. The seller was obviously pleased but said, that as he had not yet bought the consignment, it would be best to keep it intact until the deal was concluded, however, not to be concerned as under no circumstances would he return the coins that my friend wished. My friend agreed, very unhappy to leave the coins behind, but feeling that if he insisted upon taking them away under the circumstances he might arouse the suspicions of the seller and jeopardize the sale. So he went home and returned early the next morning to pick up his purchase. The merchant was ready for him, handing him a freshly smelted silver bar and telling him that, to show his appreciation for the kindness and generosity, he had come early to his shop, melted down the coins into a brick of shiny silver metal as in that form it would be more convenient for my friend to use in making whatever he had in mind! The only pleasant feature of the incident that I can record is that my friend did not drop dead from apoplexy on the spot!

In addition to the examples of the regal coinage of the early Macedonian kings, Alexander I, Philip II, and Alexander III, that appeared more or less frequently in the Istanbul Bazaar in the 1930s, one saw less frequently, but occasionally, coins from some Macedonian and Thracian cities. Among these were Mende, Aenus, and Abdera.

But it was in Athens one summer evening, while sipping the local resinated white wine with friends on the terrace of the old casino at Glyfada, that someone said, "You should have a coin of Mende. Those people raised good grapes and made good wine, and knew how to enjoy life. They put a drunken Dionysus on their coins." I found several, but the one I eventually bought was the one nobody wanted. It had been lightly double struck and as a result the body of Dionysus, his arm and the cantharos he holds is shown double, as if moving, while the head of the donkey is sharp and clear. It seemed to me that the unplanned, unwanted accident in striking really heightened the interest in the coin, which shows a drunken Dionysus, holding a cantharos, reclining on the back of his donkey. The reverse of the coin shows a grapevine in an incuse square surrounded by the name of the city. Later I was to find finer examples of Mende coins in the Istanbul Bazaar but the coin that I always liked the best was the one that I first purchased.

Aenus, an important Thracian city at the mouth of the Hebrus river, began to mint money about 470 B.C. Its early coins show a head of Hermes in profile wearing a tight-fitting petasos. On the reverse is a standing goat, the name of the city, and a symbol in an incuse square. In later coins the head of Hermes is facing. A facing head is a challenge to the greatest of the die-makers. Cimon, the Syracusan engraver, succeeded at this above all other men, and in antiquity, as today, his tetradrachms with the facing head of Arethusa are among the most admired of all coins. The facing head was used at times in many mints, among them Aenus, Apollonia Pontica, Amphipolis, Athens, Clazomenae, Cyzicus, Istrus, Larissa, Rhodes, Syracuse, and Tarsus.

Teos was a city in Ionia not far from Izmir. When the advance of the armies of the Great King came out of Persia to threaten their land, the people of Teos preferred exile to life under the Persian rule. So the entire population moved from their own city and occupied an abandoned site on the Thracian coast near the Nestus River called Abdera. Here, about 540 B.C., they brought out their first coinage, copied from that of their home city. The obverse shows a seated griffin with rounded wing and one paw raised. There was usually a symbol below the griffin. The reverse was a shallow incuse square divided into four parts and, in later issues, the name of a magistrate in the frame of the incuse. History records that the Persian King Xerxes in his advance into Greece chose Abdera, by then a prosperous city, for a rest stop, which nicely illustrates the Oriental proverb that you cannot avoid your fate.

It seemed that we Americans were just out of the financial depression of the 1930s when we all had very little extra cash, and then into World War II when we had even less money for extravagances, and little time. In 1942-44 I was back on duty in Istanbul, working with a highly competent and enthusiastic young staff on a program of expanded reporting. The work-load was very heavy, and on many days after closing the office at the end of a long day's work and before beginning the night's home work, my relaxation was to walk from Beyoglu to Stambul and tour the Bazaars, often in the company of Consul William Fraleigh, and that was pleasant. The merchant-buyers from England and Switzerland were absent from the market and foreign collectors generally had ceased their activities for the duration of the war. One prominent exception was Mr. Calouste Gulbenkian. Mr. Gulbenkian was born in Istanbul and as a boy had haunted the Grand Bazaar searching for ancient coins. As a man he left Turkey but maintained his interest in coins. His buying agent for coins in Istanbul was Mr. S. Heim. Because of Mr. Gulbenkian's excellent connections, vast wealth, and many nationalities, Mr. Heim was always able to send him fine coins. Once in discussing coins and the war years with Mr. Gulbenkian I asked him, perhaps indiscreetly, just what was his citizenship, and he replied "that of the country where I am residing unless at the time I am a diplomatic officer of another country."

During the war years several large hoards appeared in Istanbul, which Fraleigh and I had the opportunity to examine, and we acquired some fine coins. One particularly interesting find was of several thousand tetradrachms found near Ezine and containing in large part the coins of Antigonus Gonatas and Antigonus Doson. But before considering these it will be more orderly to look briefly at the careers and the coinage of the immediate ancestors of these kings.

The Satrap Antigonus was one of the generals and heirs of Alexander the Great. After Alexander's death Antigonus continued to strike coins of the type and in the name of Alexander. He had a son, Demetrius, who fought with distinction, although not always with success, in support of his father. In the defense of the southern boundaries of his father's empire Demetrius lost at Gaza to Ptolemy and Seleucus in 321 B.C., and the same year he was unsuccessful against Seleucus in Babylonia. In 307 he liberated Athens from Cassander's garrison and was deified by the grateful Athenians. The next year he defeated Ptolemy in a naval battle off Salamis on Cyprus. After the victory, Antigonus for the first time called himself "king," and he bestowed the title on Demetrius. In 305, Demetrius besieged Rhodes with skill and vigor but in the end unsuccessfully, and thereafter he was known as Poliorcetes or the Besieger. He fought Cassander victoriously in Greece, but was summoned soon thereafter to his father's aid in Asia where in 301 they were disastrously defeated at Ipsus. Antigonus perished in the battle, but Demetrius survived, with the fleet intact and a few bases loyal to him. His own genius and the quarreling of his adversaries among themselves permitted him to re-emerge in a few years as a major force. But Pyrrhus and Lysimachus drove him out of Macedonia and he moved into Asia where, after experiencing heavy desertions from his land army and the loss of contact with his fleet, he surrendered to Seleucus in 285, dying in honorable captivity two years later. I esteem Demetrius' loyalty to his father, I admire his dash and verve and military genius, and I like his coinage, but it is perhaps best to close the story here on a note of admiration, than to read further, for as one biographer put it: "In a life full of scandal he collected wives and mistresses and gaily defied all convention in the pursuit of his pleasures."

The early gold staters of Demetrius were on the model of the staters of Alexander with the head of Athena on the obverse, and a Nike on the reverse but with the name of Demetrius replacing that of Alexander. One type of tetradrachm shows on the obverse a Nike blowing a trumpet and holding a naval standard on the prow of a ship. The reverse shows Poseidon wielding a trident, the name of Demetrius the King, and a monogram and letter. The type refers to Demetrius' naval victory at Salamis. Mr. Barkley Head noted that the same victory is commemorated by a monument discovered on the island of Samothrace, now in the Louvre, consisting of a Nike standing on a prow, as on the coins. The theory of a relationship between the coins and the statue is no longer generally accepted, and, probably definitely outdated by new finds discovered in excavations at Samothrace. A second type shows the diademed and horned head of Demetrius on the obverse, and on the reverse Poseidon resting his foot on rocks and leaning on a trident with the name of Demetrius the King and various monograms. Occasionally Poseidon is shown seated on rocks and holding an aplustre and a trident. Demetrius' coins were the first portrait coins issued in Europe.

Antigonus Gonatas, son of Demetrius Poliorcetes, was left in charge in Greece when Demetrius made his final bid in Asia to regain his Empire. Antigonus took the title of King upon the death of his father in 283 B.C. He allied himself with Antiochus by marriage with Antiochus' daughter, Phila, but even with this powerful support he did not have an easy time. At various times, and sometimes in combination, he was attacked by Pyrrhus, Lysimachus, Ptolemy, and a disloyal lieutenant, but fate and his energy helped him and he died in control of much of his Empire. He defeated the Egyptian fleet at the battle of Cos, thereby winning control of the Aegean Sea. His coin types commemorate this victory.

Tetradrachm of Antigonus Gonatas (277-239 B.C.).

Antigonus was a cultivated man who encouraged arts and was himself a friend of Zeno, the founder of Stoicism.

The obverse of Antigonus' tetradrachms show a Macedonian shield in the center of which is a head of Pan, horned, with a pedium at his shoulder. According to some authors this is actually a portrait of Antigonus. The reverse shows Athena Alkis of archaistic style hurling a fulmen and holding a shield. The name of Antigonus the King is there, usually with a Macedonian helmet and a monogram. In the 1940s these coins seemed quite expensive at twenty dollars each!

At his death in 240 B.C., Antigonus Gonatas was succeeded by his son Demetrius II who reigned for about ten years. At his death in 229 B.C., he was succeeded by his son Philip V, who was still a child. Antigonus Doson, like Philip, a grandson of Antigonus Gonatas, was appointed guardian of the young Philip. Doson fought off foreign invaders and regained some separated parts of the kingdom. He only assumed the title of King when the army threatened revolt. His coin types probably commemorate his naval victory in 228 in a war against Caria. He died in 221 B.C., leaving the throne to Philip and the country more stable and strong than it had been for many years.

The silver tetradrachms of Antigonus Doson show on the obverse the head of Poseidon with flowing hair and beard and a wreath of seaweed around his head; on the reverse, Apollo, nude, seated on the prow of a vessel inscribed "King Antigonus." There is considerable variation in the style of these coins, but I like them all. I admire the splendid head of Poseidon and the graceful Apollo. In fact I think of the coins of Antigonus Doson as one of the finest issues of Hellenistic coinage.

Tetradrachm of Antigonus Doson (229-220 B.C.).

Ancient Greek Coins

I was sitting one afternoon in George Zacos' shop talking with George and Aziz Bey, who was making one of his checks of the market, when a man from Antalya came in and offered George a magnificent gold medallion which he said he had found in the sea. It was a large Ptolemaic coin struck in Egypt and likely brought to Antalya by some important person about the time that Cleopatra came there on her tryst with Mark Antony. George examined the coin and handed it to me. I admired it and handed it to Aziz Bey, saying that I would like to purchase it if he did not wish it for the Museum. He replied: "We have the coin in the museum and it is not our wish to acquire every coin that is found. If a coin is unique, we want it for the museum; if it is rare, and we do not have it, we want it. But if we already have one or more examples of it then we do not want it; we do not have the administrative or curatorial staff to take care of everything. Moreover, Turkey is glad to have the foreign exchange that you bring here to buy old coins. And we are pleased to see these little objects go into foreign museums where they are silent propagandists inviting people to visit Turkey and spend their money to see the wonders of our land. After all, coins were made to circulate, and that is just what they are doing when collectors buy them." After Aziz Bey departed, serious bargaining began for the coin. I did not get it—it was too expensive, but George purchased it for some more affluent collector. But I did not go away empty handed. George, as was his custom in such circumstances, sold me a coin as a consolation prize, this time a tetradrachm of Philip V, which in any other circumstance would have been considered a grand prize.

As the young new king, Philip took the field against his enemies and won. Within four years he had overthrown the council of guardians set up by Doson. In this time, Macedonia first challenged Rome. Philip was defeated. He then collaborated loyally with Rome and prospered. He issued a new currency and when he died in 179 B.C. he left his throne to his son Perseus. The tetradrachm of Philip George sold me shows the head of the king diademed and slightly bearded on the obverse. On the reverse is Athena Alkis armed with a shield and hurling a fulmen, with the name of the king and two monograms.

Tetradrachm of Philip V (220-179 B.C.).

Perseus reigned for eleven years. He had inherited a full treasury and a strong army, but he failed to appreciate the dawning power of Rome in the East and to apply all his ample resources to curb it. The result was that with a full treasury he lost the battle of Pydna to the Romans, and from that time Macedonia ceased to be an independent kingdom. The tetradrachms of Perseus are magnificent portraits. On the obverse they show the head of the king, slightly bearded, and on the reverse an eagle on a fulmen with the name of the king, all within an oak wreath. A hoard of several hundred Perseus tetradrachms surfaced in the Bazaar in 1942 from which I chose a few pieces at fifty Turkish liras each, about twenty dollars at the time.

And here, while our thoughts are on the successors of Alexander, we should consider two other lines of successors, Lysimachus and the Seleucids. Theodore Zumbulakis used to say that the coins of Lysimachus were the favorite coins of the Americans. In his shop, I have watched him prove his statement many times. When a stranger, who was an American, would come in and ask for coins, Theodore would lay out on a tray a dozen coins and offer them for examination. In nine cases out of ten, the Lysimachus coin would be the one first picked up by the American customer. They have always appealed to me. They are fine coins, comfortably heavy in the hand, often with a splendid head in high relief, a pleasant historical association with Alexander the Great—and they were available in abundance. They should be a favorite of the British, too, for the reverse type was the prototype of the "Britannia rules the waves" series of English coins.

Illustrated, on page 186 are a series of gold staters of Lysimachus, bought individually at various places and times. Anyone of them could have come out of the Istanbul Bazaar, but only the last two did, being selected from a small hoard that was available in 1942. Also shown are a series of silver tetradrachms, struck in the name of Lysimachus at various of his mints during his lifetime and after his death. Alexander died in 323 B.C.; at the time Lysimachus was Regent of Thrace. For some time he

Tetradrachm of Lysimachus (323-281 B.C.).

continued to strike coins of the type and in the name of Alexander. About 305 B.C., he assumed the title of King and a few years later began to strike coins, only substituting his name for Alexander's on the old types in some issues, but for most mints using his name on a new type. I bought my first specimen of this coinage in Athens and later continued the series in Istanbul or wherever I found what I needed.

After I had retired from the Foreign Service and built a house on the hills overlooking the Bosphorus, I returned to Istanbul for a few months each year and on these excursions I visited the Bazaar almost every day always calling at George's shop. George was active and hospitable. He subscribed to many numismatic and archaeological reviews. His library was one of the best specialized private libraries in the city. The ambiance of the shop, plus the certainty of seeing new material there, made it a meeting-place for local personalities, serious students, professors, numismatists, archaeologists, visiting celebrities, and just friends. In the course of time one could be sure to meet there, in a relaxed atmosphere, anyone interested in the art of the past. George sold me several coins in my Seleucid series, but most of the Seleucid coins came onto the market from Beirut, not Istanbul.

Seleucus inherited or won the greatest part of Alexander's Empire. He and his successors struck a long series of coins which are in fact an excellent portrait gallery from Hellenistic times. While considering Hellenistic portraits one must not overlook the realistic portrait of Philetaerus on the coinage of his successors. He looks like a tough character and, perhaps because he was, King Lysimachus selected him to guard the royal treasure of nine thousand talents which the King deposited at Pergamum. But Philetaerus proved tougher than Lysimachus had anticipated for in 284 B.C. he declared himself independent and reigned until 263. He was succeeded by his nephew Eumenes, and on his death, after a reign of twenty-five years, by another nephew, Attalus I. Illustrated on page 187 is a tetradrachm of this king showing on the obverse a laureate head of Philetaerus and on the reverse Athena, seated holding a spear with her shield behind her. She is crowning the name of Philetaerus.

To end this series of Hellenistic portraits, I wish to call attention to three portraits from the dynasty of the Kings of Bithynia and one from the dynasty of the Kings of Pontus. From Bithynia I chose Prusius I, the fourth king, who reigned for about fifty years. The portraits here from tetradrachms, show him as a young man. On the obverse is the diademed head of the king, with face slightly bearded; on the reverse is Zeus, standing with sceptre and crowning the name of the king. From Pontus, I chose Mithridates VI because his life story delights me. The coins of Mithridates VI show the head of Mithridates on the obverse and a stag feeding, the king's name, date of issue, a crescent and star, and monograms, all within an ivy wreath, on the reverse. The two silver coins illustrated here are very similar in design.

Mithridates VI, known as the Great, was indeed an extraordinary man by any standard. He was born in the Greek city of Sinope in Pontus, the eldest son of King Mithridates V. He grew up among the Greek youth of Sinope. He was a self-willed boy who was proud that he was an Achaemenid, a royal Persian, and a descendent of the Great King. He wore Persian clothing, a long-sleeved tunic, baggy trousers caught at the ankle, and an embroidered belt which held a dagger. His father was assassinated when he was eight years old and his mother became Queen-Regent. At that time it was not unusual for a regent to slowly poison the heir so that he would die of apparently natural causes before he could claim his inheritance. This routine, sanctioned by custom, was tried on young Mithridates, but when he noted an odd flavor to his food he knew what to do about it. He regularly took an antidote and then a small amount of poison to test the antidote. This daily regime he started as a youth and continued until his dying day, long deferred because of it.

Tetradrachm of Mithridates VI (120-63 B.C.).

The warning was enough. So, with a few carefully chosen friends, he, at the age of fourteen, set off on a hunting expedition with food for a few days, not to turn up again until seven years later. During this time he lived in the mountain forests, changing his camp site each night, eating the game that he captured, and occasionally visiting the castle of some vassal lord to replace his horses or clothing. In these years he grew tall, strong, and handsome, and was admitted to be the finest horseman and the truest shot in all Asia. When he was twenty-one he appeared, without prior notice, in the marketplace of Sinope, and announced that he had come to claim his inheritance. His good looks and oratory won the crowd over and they marched on the Palace. The Queen-Regent submitted and was exiled. Mithridates married his sister, which was eminently respectable in those days since the royal family was so distinguished that there was no family in all the world sufficiently exalted to marry into it!

Mithridates started a family, consolidated his position, increased his strength, went traveling to learn the weaknesses of Rome, returned home, learned that his sister-wife had plotted against him in his absence, and promptly murdered her along with a large number of her courtiers. Then, when Romans were occupied by events in Rome, he enlarged his kingdom through diplomacy, conquest, and trickery. The story is told that in the war against his nephew, the King of Cappadocia, the two armies fought to a draw. A truce was arranged so that the two Kings could talk together. The opposing armies occupied the two sides of a great plain. The two Kings each with a small cavalry escort moved toward each other and halted. Each King was searched for concealed weapons, the escorts returned and the two Kings, in the sight of everyone but within the hearing of none, moved toward each other. Mithridates, before the meeting, and with nobody knowing of it, had strapped a very sharp little knife to his penis, and this was not noticeable under his baggy Persian trousers. Then, when he was close enough to embrace his nephew, Mithridates pulled out his weapon and cut his nephew's throat from ear to ear—and another day's work was done!

When he was ready, he attacked the Romans, won, and pushed them out of Asia. To the Greek population he was a hero and the liberator of Hellas. To understand this one must remember that the Romans were regarded by the Greeks of Asia Minor as barbarians who offered nothing but came only to rape the land.

Mithridates went from triumph to disaster and back but he always survived to start again. At times he took desperate chances, as for example, when, fleeing by sea from the armies of Lucullus, his ship became waterlogged and he transferred himself and his war chest to a pirate ship. The pirates could have delivered him to the Romans, and been paid handsomely, but instead they delivered him to his own safe harbor. Such was his personal magnetism and luck when dealing with rascals. On a later occasion, when defeated and abandoned, and forced to fly from his kingdom, without even horses to carry his baggage, he was faced with the problem of transporting his vast treasure of gold and silver. He solved this by dividing it among his soldiers, paying each soldier a year's wage in advance, and each officer a correspondingly larger sum. Thus the treasure was transported, and such was the loyalty of his men that on a march of many months not a single soldier deserted with the silver that he was carrying.

At sixty-nine, Mithridates, far from his homeland, attacked by his son, deserted by all but his castle guard, a fugitive from his own kingdom and a rebel in Roman eyes, saw his day was over. He took a lethal dose of poison, but it did not work as he was immune because of the antidote that he had taken regularly for nearly sixty years. In desperation he ordered a faithful chieftain to take his life. He died with pride. He had lived with honor as it was understood at the time. It was honorable for him, for example, to order that all his women be killed, each in the manner she chose, rather than risk that they fall into enemy hands. He was brave, generous, and chivalrous. He had great personal magnetism that kept the loyalty of his soldiers even in defeat through many years. He used the accepted methods of his day to maintain his position. In short, he was a man of his time.

The "owls" of Athens were a very popular international currency in the late sixth century and throughout the fifth century B.C. They continued to circulate in Asia Minor in reduced numbers during the centuries that followed. The Athenian was the earliest currency with a head as a type and one of the first with obverse and reverse types. The early issues show on the obverse an almond-eyed Athena with an archaic smile and an unadorned helmet. On the reverse is an owl, an olive twig, and three letters indicating the source of the money. Coins issued after the battles of Marathon and Salamis carried three upright olive leaves along the front of Athena's helmet and a waning moon beside the olive twig on the reverse. The type remained substantially unchanged, although as time passed the archaic smile faded, the eye became less frontal and more in profile, and the engravers of new dies did what they could to modernize their dies while working within the framework of a fixed convention. I often am asked, "Why the owl?" I suppose the reason is it was Athena's bird, as the dove was sacred to Aphrodite and the eagle to Zeus.

The coins of Athens have always been special favorites of mine, and I have been very fortunate in acquiring them. Through the thoughtfulness of two friends in Cairo, Mr. Joseph Khawan and Mr. Phocian Tano, I had the opportunity of seeing, and choosing from, seven thousand Athenian coins of the Tell-el-Mashkuta hoard soon after it was discovered in the mid-1940s. Shortly after that three hoards of archaic Greek coins, including many Athenians, were found in Turkey, but as the Athenian coins from these hoards offered nothing new for my collection I bought none. There was also found about the same time in Turkey a fourth-century hoard of Athenian coinage. Some of these coins, at least, were struck locally at the time and included, along with countermarks, some interesting variations, as, for example, when the obverse and reverse types were kept intact but the ethnic was totally changed. Found in this hoard was a single tetradrachm with the portrait bust of the Satrap replacing the head of Athena. I saw the coin in Istanbul but I could not get it as the dealer-owner had already offered it to the British Museum, whose keeper of coins later was to describe it as the most important numismatic discovery of our time. Although I missed this unique coin, I owned two decadrachms and many other Athenian rarities, as well as thirty-seven archaic tetradrachms that came much later from the Delta hoard. Illustrated here on page 190 are a series of Athens tetradrachms most of which came from documented hoards not found in Turkey. Anyone of them could have come out of the Istanbul Bazaar where, during my collecting days, I saw many similar coins. On the plate on page 190, the first row, with reverses

Tetradrachm of Athens of the early fifth century B.C.

below, shows coins of the sixth century B.C.; the third row, coins of the early fifth century; the fifth row, coins of the mid-fifth century; and the seventh row, coins of the late fifth century. At times the demand for Athens silver coins must have been greater than the supply for they were imitated in antiquity in Asia Minor. The last two coins on the plate are two such imitations where the essential features of the type are maintained but the details altered. Note, for example, in the second from the last coin the owl is standing left rather than right, and the ethnic appears in the left, rather than the right field. In the final coin a local name and alphabet is used in place of the Greek.

I was, if anything, too lucky with ancient coins. A splendid specimen would come into my hands and I would blithely give it away without a tinge of regret to some interested person as I was confident that it would soon be replaced by another coin equally as interesting. In the Near East, I was somewhat like the European immigrant to America who, soon after arriving, found a twenty-dollar gold piece on the street and with a shrug of the shoulders handed it to a friend because "the streets of America are paved with gold." But in my case, during the years I was an active collector, the curious fact was that the coin I gave away was soon replaced by something just as interesting!

On a visit to the Istanbul Bazaar in 1952 (I was working in Washington at the time) one of the three merchants then active in antique coins asked me if I would care to buy some Aspendus staters. Since in the Orient it is always well when buying to dissimulate your enthusiasm, I replied that I would agree to give my time to look at the coins if he recommended them. He immediately consented, fixing an appointment for the following day, as the coins were being studied by an unnamed collector at the time. The hoard, or more accurately the section of the hoard, as one part of it had already gone to the Istanbul Museum, was really impressive. It consisted of several thousand Aspendus silver coins in beautiful condition. While I am not a particular admirer of the coinage of Aspendus, this hoard contained some very interesting obverse variations and an intriguing series of symbols on the reverse. Note, for example, the different positions of the hands and feet in the series shown on page 191. I selected some thirty pieces for my collection at six Turkish liras each (then about three dollars), and was assured that I was the second collector to choose from the hoard. Later I learned that other collectors had seen those coins before I had looked at them. One was Mr. Hans von Aulock who has assembled, and now published in eighteen volumes, a most remarkable—and perhaps the finest in existence—series of coins of Asia Minor in a single collection. Numismatists over the world, those now living, and those who will follow, owe a great debt of gratitude to Mr. von Aulock for his industry, research, writings, and perseverance.

Another hoard, or section of a hoard (one is never very sure when he is shown a bag of ancient coins if what he sees is the entire find because very often the find is divided at the time of discovery and reaches the market in sections) that came to the Istanbul Bazaar in the early 1950s was made up of Satrapal coins from Tarsus.

Tarsus was the most important city of Cilicia. Coins were struck there by the Satraps of the Great King. Illustrated on page 191 are two early coins of Tarsus. They are silver staters of Persian weight. The inscription is in Aramaic. On the obverse many coins show Baaltars (Zeus to the Greeks) seated, or a female head, likely copied from the Arethusa of Cimon. On the reverse is a helmeted male head, perhaps Ares or the Satrap, or, toward the end of the series, the God Ana, and, perhaps the Satrap standing facing to either side of a thymiaterion. On the third from the last coin in this series is a lion attacking a bull. The reverse of the next coin shows two lines of walls each with four towers with the animals above. In this series the clarity of detail, especially the heads of the small figures, is noteworthy, as well as the variation in detail, for example, in the ornamentation of the helmets.

I have always liked the large flan Hellenistic coins struck in Asia Minor, although at the time that I was buying they were not popular among the "experts" who favored the archaic series. But because the Hellenistic coins were not stylish then they were cheap, and so my collection grew. On pages 189-191 are shown a series of coins from the island of Tenedos and the Aeolian and Ionian cities of Aegae, Cyme, Myrina, Smyrna, and Magnesia. I selected these specimens from among others which the Istanbul dealer said had been a part of a huge hoard. I was told that the three brothers who had found the hoard had traded their find to a landowner for land for their daughters' dowries, and the landowner had then traded the coins to an Istanbul antiquarian for an apartment in the city. It was interesting to me that ancient coins could continue to serve as a medium of exchange in modern times. This fact was lately brought home by the news story, in December, 1972, that the Metropolitan Museum of New York had purchased a magnificent Ancient Greek vase paying for it in part with antique coins. I had also heard while working in Athens in 1940 when the money of the moment had depreciated to near zero, that one could legally purchase bread with antique Athens coins, but I never put the story to the test. As a footnote to this series of coins I may add that in 1972 I saw in Turkey and in Europe sections of a newly found hoard, totaling nearly two thousand coins, many in mint condition, from these same cities, but I bought none.

The coins of the little Greek island of Tenedos intrigue me, primarily because I have been able to obtain so little accurate information about them. They carry a Janiform head, male and female, on the obverse, and a double ax, the name of the island, a bunch of grapes, and a symbol, all within a laurel wreath on the reverse. It has been suggested that the two heads are of Zeus and Hera. It has also been suggested that the double ax, always accompanied by a bunch of grapes, is a cult object of Dionysus.

Aegae, a town of Aeolis, inland from the sea, struck coins in the second century B.C., and perhaps even into the first century, that, like the Tenedos coins, had a large flan. On the obverse of these coins is a laureate head of Apollo with bow and quiver at his shoulder. On the reverse is a figure of Zeus, naked, standing holding an eagle and sceptre all within an oak wreath.

Cyme, according to one legend, was founded by the Amazon Cyme. At any rate it was one of the oldest and noblest of the Aeolian cities. It had rich farming land. Its coin types in the mid-second century B.C. show a head, which may be that of the Amazon, on the obverse, and on the reverse a horse standing with one foreleg raised, the name of the town, and a magistrate's name all within a laurel wreath.

Myrina, like Cyme, was an Aeolian city. Here, Apollo of Grynium was worshiped. On the coins of Myrina shown on page 189 there is a head of Apollo of Grynium on the obverse. On the reverse is a standing figure of Apollo of Grynium, in himation, holding a phiale and laurel branch. In front of him are an omphalos and an amphora. The omphalos refers to the existence of an oracle at the temple of Apollo at Grynium, about four miles from Myrina.

At about the same time Smyrna in Ionia issued a coin with an obverse showing a lady with a turreted crown. This is the head of Cybele; on the reverse is the name of the city and monogram of a magistrate's name all within an oak wreath.

Magnesia ad Maeandrum, south and east of Smyrna, had been from earliest times a city of considerable importance. In 190 B.C. it began striking coins with the head of Artemis on the obverse, and Apollo standing left on a maeander pattern leaning his elbow on a tripod, on the reverse.

Facing, or three-quarters facing, heads, as I have indicated, pose highly difficult problems for the die-maker, but when they succeed really splendid coins result. Such are the early coins of Rhodes. About

408 B.C., the three independent ancient towns of Camirus, Ialysus, and Lindus on the island of Rhodes combined to form a new city, Rhodes, which became the capital of the island and the center of life of that very prosperous maritime state. As the people of the island claimed descent from Helios, the sun-god, they chose as the obverse type of their coinage the head of this god, facing, and the rose as the reverse type, which in Greek is *rhodos*. Also in honor of Helios the Rhodians set up their Colossus, one of the wonders of the ancient world. On the last plate (page 192) are two examples of the early Rhodian coinage and one example of the later coinage where the head is radiate. In medieval times people believed that these latter coins were the Biblical thirty pieces of silver and the coins represented the head of Christ wearing the crown of thorns. The silver coins of Rhodes ceased to be issued in the middle of the first century before Christ. In 1970 a hoard of about one hundred early Rhodian coins, some of them of splendid style and excellent preservation, was uncovered near Marmaris in Turkey and found its way directly to the European market. I saw it there, admired it, but was not tempted. I was no longer collecting and the prices asked were fantastically high, or so they seemed to an old collector.

The Satraps of Caria, vassals of the Great King, issued from their capital city, Halicarnassus, a series of attractive silver tetradrachms showing on the obverse the head of Apollo, laureate and facing. The reverse shows Zeus Labraundos, armed with a spear and double ax, walking right, and the name of the Satrap (Mausolus, Hidrieus, or Pixodarus). This coinage ended with the conquest of Asia Minor by Alexander the Great. The tomb of Mausolus, called the Mausoleum of Halicarnassus, was one of the seven wonders of the ancient world.

Several years ago I read that certain speculators in Milan, realizing that the prices of modern paintings were advancing rapidly, and would likely continue to advance rapidly, began buying paintings by current big-name artists and putting them away in a "silo" to be sold later at a handsome profit. I did not know that the same procedure was being applied to the coin market until I saw a variation of it with my own eyes. On that occasion I was waiting in the outer office of one of the world's leading numismatists when a young man, fashionably dressed and well mannered, came in and requested to see some "good" coins. He was asked what type of coins he had in mind, and he replied it really did not matter so long as they were attractive. He was shown some thalers from which he chose a few, then some Roman deniers which he rejected as being insignificant. He asked for gold and chose several Roman aurii and a few Greek staters without looking at them closely or even inquiring the price. Then he hesitated, and, because I was intrigued, I said to him, "You should not neglect the Greek silver for it is the most beautiful of all." He replied, "You really think so?" and when I nodded he asked for Greek silver, choosing, and, occasionally asking my opinion, from the coins in the series that he was shown. When he finished I said to him, "You have asked my help and I gave it gladly, and now will you satisfy my curiosity? Just what are you doing?" He replied, "I am in the business of making money fast legitimately. I have just now bought ancient coins from a world-famous dealer for 25,000 Swiss Francs. I take two invoices, one is sealed in the envelope with the coins. The other I will carry in my pocket. Tomorrow I will call on one of several persons that I know in Geneva who are making great sums of money overnight and say, 'Here is a package of choice ancient gold and silver coins that I have just bought from a famous dealer. Coin prices have increased in value, as you know, fantastically over recent months and there is every prospect that they will continue to increase. Here is the receipted invoice and a duplicate is sealed in the package with the coins. You can have the package at a twenty percent profit.' And," he added, "I will sell the package easily without it being opened!"

Certainly such activities tend to increase prices but the greatest boost in prices has come from the public auctions, sometimes to the utter confusion of merchants and old collectors alike. I heard recently that a certain aurius was sold at an auction in Switzerland for more than fifteen thousand dollars when a like coin in as good condition was for months previously in a tray of a prominent dealer with a price tag of seven hundred dollars! Formerly a collector, or several collectors, might run up the price of a coin to a new high at an auction, but there was always a point beyond which bidders did not go, and there was a valid reason for the high bidding. But today there seems to be no limit, and I can see no reason behind some of the bids made for ancient coins. Of course this trend is not new, but it has become greatly accentuated of late. One of my good friends, Mr. Nicholas Karageorge, left Istanbul some ten years ago, and in 1965, I wrote him, "...I very much miss meeting you in the Bazaars here, but if you were visiting them today you would find them much changed from three years ago. In the first place George, Niko, and Petro (Bazaar antique dealers) have immigrated elsewhere; some of the merchants who replaced them now make regular trips to Europe and they save their better purchases for these trips; while many of the small merchants from southern Turkey are going to Beirut to dispose of their accumulations. Most important, prices on the local market have risen until they are higher for some things than European prices for corresponding things. Nevertheless, I continue to visit the Bazaars when I am in Istanbul, but now for distraction, like one goes to a movie, rather than for the opportunity to improve my collections."

If I were to write my friend today on the same subject I would be hard pressed to find adjectives to describe to what extent prices of antique coins have risen!

In my Numismatic Biography, privately printed in 1970 for my friends, I wrote that by the late 1950s a new and strong trend was developing that concerned every collector of ancient coins living in the Near or Middle East. First, prices were rising rapidly. Coins that I had purchased in the 1930s for $50 each were selling at public auctions in Switzerland in 1970 at $1000 each. Accordingly what had once been fun to buy now became a serious financial transaction. With prices everywhere on the rise forgeries were planted in the villages in increasing numbers and some of these were quite well made. Then, "innocent" farmers brought their "new finds" to the city where merchants and collectors often found it difficult at a glance to tell the good from the fake. And, more important, the attitude in the Near Eastern countries toward collectors was changing. Where formerly everybody was eager to help the foreign collector, people now were becoming suspicious, and even envious, that you, the foreign collector, saw value in objects in which they saw no value. Newspapers began to give prominence to stories of inflated prices that some antique objects brought abroad, and it was then but a step for the ignorant to accuse collectors of accumulating the wealth of the nation!

Certainly, there is a genuine grievance where newly discovered major works of art are exported without authorization or where farmers are encouraged to dig for treasure on archaeological sites on their land. However, many people overreacted to the existing situation and urged the absolute prohibition of collecting any form of antiquity by private persons. But it always seemed to me to be a mistake to prohibit, or make extremely difficult, the collection or exportation of all antiquities, and particularly such mass-produced minor objects as coins. To do so would in effect put an end to the activities of every conscientious local collector, and would curtail private research, and gifts of duplicate coins to museums from private collectors. It would also mean, where severe laws were passed, that the trade in coins would go underground, and newly found hoards would be exported without being seen locally, thereby depriving local museums of their greatest source of acquisition—the confiscation of segments of hoards. Nevertheless, in spite of such considerations, the trend was clearly developing in the late 1950s to limit the activities of private collectors and therefore, with the end of an epoch in sight, it seemed to me to be the time to bring an end to my collecting. By this time, too, many old friends who were officials had retired, and their replacements, regardless of their private feelings, were sensitive to this new trend and found it expedient to go along with it.

Thus changing circumstances heavily influenced my decision to become an inactive collector, for a collection that is no longer growing, and which could not grow in this environment, is really lifeless. Therefore, in 1958, I showed my collection of ancient Greek coins at the American Numismatic Society in New York and said to Miss Margaret Thompson, the Curator of Greek Coins: "Choose as a gift to the Society any coin that you do not have now in the Society's trays and any coin that is in a better state than the example that you now have in your trays." Miss Thompson, with her colleagues, chose 1506 gold, electrum, and silver coins, and in 1962 the Society published a carefully prepared and beautifully presented Sylloge of them in two volumes. From the remainder of my collection I gave a representative series to the Museum of Art at Indiana University, a large series of Alexander the Great tetradrachms to the Art Institute of Chicago, and many smaller groups of individual coins to colleagues, friends, and people who had been helpful to me in my thirty years of active collecting. I was content. I had had my fun, and I had satisfaction in placing all that was important where it could be admired and studied by any interested person, for, after all, few people today would be likely to have the opportunities that I had had in collecting.

Now, more than a decade since I stopped serious collecting, I continue to feel satisfied with my decision. In Turkey, where I enjoy passing several months each year, I observed the pressure build up to replacing the old Ottoman law on antiquities. Talking with my Turkish friends I suggested taking a good look at the Lebanese law on the subject. There a licensed antique dealer can sell an antique for export, but must first show the object at the local museum giving the facts of the sale. If the authorities choose, they can buy the object at the declared selling price. If they do not buy, they must grant an export license, the merchant paying an export tax according to a sliding scale. This brings considerable revenue to the museum and considerable foreign exchange to Lebanon. I also urged a study of the American law that permits the donors of objects to museums to deduct from their income taxes, according to established rules, the actual market value of the donations. The holdings of American museums have increased enormously through this provision of the law. Finally, in the autumn of 1973, a new Turkish law was published. It is a harsh law perhaps designed primarily to end commercial smuggling. It does permit local collectors to continue to collect under certain conditions, but it prohibits exportation on a commercial basis or as gifts to foreign museums. Very seldom is there the opportunity to make a significant contribution by the gift of an ancient coin to the holdings of the local museum since its trays are fantastically rich. So there remains little incentive for the foreign numismatist in Turkey to collect ancient coins.

To close this chapter and this book, I choose to use a coin from Colophon not so much for the beauty of the coin as for its significance. Colophon was a city in Ionia situated about twenty miles north and west of Ephesus. In antiquity it was famous for the excellence of its cavalry. When a battle was at its height, or at that critical moment between victory and defeat, the cavalry of Colophon would storm in and bring victory. It was unrivaled, the last word, in what it represented. Because of this, publishers began long ago to put a final symbol or mark at the end of their work. They called this "the Colophon." It seems appropriate to me, therefore, that I end this book with a coin of Colophon, a town that ceased to exist in 299 B.C. but which has left us something that is meaningful today.

Plates for Chapter VIII

Almost all of the coins illustrated here are in the trays of the American Numismatic Society of New York. They were photographed by the Society's photographer in 1954 and 1955 and published by the Society in a Sylloge in two parts in 1961 and 1962. Some of the coins were purchased in the Grand Bazaar of Istanbul and others came through European dealers who had purchased them in the Bazaar. But all of the coins could have come out of the Bazaar, as such coins are indigenous to the area and were available in the Bazaar during the years that I was an active collector. Since this book is a general book primarily about the Bazaar, its merchants, their products and customers, rather than a series of specialized studies, the descriptions of the coins are simplified with weights, inscriptions, and monograms omitted entirely. Anyone wishing more information can refer to the Sylloge.

Page

53. 1. Asia Minor uncertain. Electron. Hecta. Sixth century.   183
    Obverse: Swastika on raised square.
    Reverse: Incuse square.
 2. Asia Minor uncertain. Electron. Hecta. Sixth century.
    Obverse: Head of Heracles.
    Reverse: Incuse square.
 3. Asia Minor uncertain. Electron. Trite. Sixth century.
    Obverse: Animal, reclining, curled into circle.
    Reverse: Oblong incuse divided into two parts.
 4. Chios. Silver. Didrachm. Sixth century.
    Obverse: Seated sphinx; to the left an amphora.
    Reverse: Incuse square.
 5. Abdera. Silver. Drachm.
    Obverse: Griffin.
    Reverse: Incuse square.
 6. Ephesus. Electron. Trite. Sixth century.
    Obverse: Bee.
    Reverse: Oblong incuse divided into two squares.
 7. Ephesus. Silver. Drachm. Sixth century.
    Obverse: Bee.
    Reverse: Incuse square.
 8. Sinope. Silver. Drachm.
    Obverse: Head of eagle, below a dolphin.
    Reverse: Incuse square with granulated surface.

9. Lydian Kings before Croesus. Electron. Trite.
   Obverse: Head of a lion.
   Reverse: Oblong incuse square.
10. Lydian Kings before Croesus. Electron. Trite.
    Obverse: Head of a lion.
    Reverse: Two incuse squares.
11. Lesbos. Electron. Hecta.
    Obverse: Lion head, right.
    Reverse: Calf's head, right, incuse.
12. Phocaea. Electron. Hecta.
    Obverse: Head of ram, right. Below, a seal.
    Reverse: Head of cock, incuse.
13. Cyzicus. Electron. Hemihecta.
    Obverse: Head of tunny.
    Reverse: Incuse square.
14. Cyzicus. Electron. Hecta.
    Obverse: Heracles wrestling with a lion, all on a tunny.
    Reverse: Incuse square.
15. Cyzicus. Electron. Hecta.
    Obverse: Panther on tunny.
    Reverse: Incuse square.
16. Phocaea. Electron. Hecta.
    Obverse: Head of griffin.
    Reverse: Incuse square.
17. Miletus. Electron. Stater.
    Obverse: Bull with head lowered.
    Reverse: oblong incuse flanked by two square incuses.
18. Croesus. Gold. Stater.
    Obverse: Foreparts of lion and bull face to face.
    Reverse: Two incuse squares side by side, one larger than the other.
19. Croesus. Gold. Light stater.
    Obverse and reverse similar to No. 18.
20. Croesus. Silver. Stater.
    Obverse and reverse similar to No.18.
21. Croesus. Silver. Half-stater.
    Obverse and reverse similar to No.18.
22. Lete. Silver. Stater.
    Obverse: Satyr and nymph.
    Reverse: Incuse square.
23. Persian Empire. Silver. Siglos.
    Obverse: King of Persia in running-kneeling attitude, holding bow and dagger.
    Reverse: Oblong incuse.
24. Persian Empire. Silver. Siglos.
    Obverse: Half figure of the King of Persia holding bow and arrows.
    Reverse: Oblong incuse.
25. Persian Empire. Silver. Siglos.
    Obverse: King of Persia kneeling, drawing a bow.
    Reverse: Oblong incuse.
26. Persian Empire. Silver. Siglos.
    Obverse: King of Persia in running-kneeling attitude, holding bow and spear.
    Reverse: Oblong incuse.

			Page
	27.	Persian Empire. Gold. Daric. Obverse: King of Persia in running-kneeling attitude, holding bow and spear. Reverse: Oblong incuse.	
	28.	Persian Empire. Gold. Double daric. Obverse: King of Persia in running-kneeling attitude, holding bow and spear. Reverse: Oblong incuse with wavy lines.	
	29.	Thasos. Silver. Stater. Obverse: Satyr ravishing a nymph. Violent style. Reverse: Incuse square.	
	30.	Thasos. Silver. Stater. Obverse: Satyr ravishing a nymph, apparently without much opposition. Reverse: Incuse square.	
	31.	Cyzicus. Electron. Stater. Obverse: Forepart of a ram; behind, tunny. Reverse: Incuse square.	
	32.	Cyzicus. Electron. Stater. Obverse: Male head, left. Below, tunny. Reverse: Incuse square.	
	33.	Cyzicus. Electron. Stater. Obverse: Griffin on tunny. Reverse: Incuse square.	
	34.	Cyzicus. Electron. Stater. Obverse: Two eagles on an omphalos, all on a tunny. Reverse: Incuse square.	
	35.	Lampsacus. Electron. Stater. Obverse: Forepart of winged horse. Reverse: Incuse square.	
54.	1.	Abdera. Silver. Tetradrachm. Obverse: Griffin. Reverse: Incuse square.	184
	2.	Abdera. Silver. Tetradrachm. Obverse: Griffin. Reverse: Incuse square.	
	3.	Abdera. Silver. Tetradrachm. Obverse: Griffin, scarabaeus, and ball. Reverse: Incuse square framed by an inscription.	
	4.	Chios. Silver. Tetradrachm. Obverse: Sphinx; to the left an amphora. Reverse: Incuse square.	
	5.	Mallus. Silver. Stater. Obverse: Winged female figure in kneeling position, holding a caduceus and wreath. Reverse: Conical baetyl with handles at top, to either side granulated patches.	
	6.	Acanthus. Silver. Tetradrachm. Obverse: Lion attacking bull; in the exergue, floral ornament. Reverse: Incuse square.	
	7.	Acanthus. Silver. Tetradrachm. Obverse: Lion attacking bull with head forward. Reverse: Incuse square.	

Page

8. Acanthus. Silver. Tetradrachm.
   Obverse: Similar.
   Reverse: Similar.
9. Acanthus. Silver. Tetradrachm.
   Obverse: Similar.
   Reverse: Incuse square framed by inscription.
10. Acanthus. Silver. Tetradrachm.
    Obverse: Similar.
    Reverse: Similar.
11. Mende. Silver. Tetradrachm.
    Obverse: Dionysus, holding cantherus, reclining on back of an ass.
    Reverse: Inscription framing vine, leaves, and grape clusters.
12. Mende. Silver. Tetradrachm.
    Obverse: Similar.
    Reverse: Similar.
13. Mende. Silver. Tetradrachm.
    Obverse: Similar.
    Reverse: Similar.
14. Mende. Silver. Tetradrachm.
    Obverse: Similar but Dionysus looking forward.
    Reverse: Similar.
15. Mende. Silver. Tetradrachm.
    Obverse: Similar.
    Reverse: Similar.
16. Alexander I. Silver. Tetradrachm.
    Obverse: Horseman carrying two spears.
    Reverse: Incuse square.
17. Alexander I. Silver. Tetradrachm.
    Obverse: Horseman, left, carrying two spears.
    Reverse: Forepart of goat, right, in incuse square.
18. Alexander I. Silver. Tetradrachm.
    Obverse: Horseman, left, carrying two spears.
    Reverse: Forepart of goat, left, in incuse square.
19. Alexander I. Silver. Tetradrachm.
    Obverse: Horseman carrying two spears.
    Reverse: Forepart of goat, right, in incuse square.
20. Alexander I. Silver. Tetradrachm.
    Obverse: Horseman carrying two spears.
    Reverse: Forepart of goat, right, head reverted, in incuse square.

55. 1. Philip II. Gold. Stater. 185
    Obverse: Laureate head of Apollo.
    Reverse: Biga with charioteer, below fulmen.
    2. Philip II. Gold. Stater.
    Obverse: Similar.
    Reverse: Similar. Below, cantherus.
    3. Philip II. Gold. Stater.
    Obverse: Similar.
    Reverse: Similar. Below, tripod.

4. Philip II. Gold. Stater.
   Obverse: Similar.
   Reverse: Similar. Below monogram.
5. Philip II. Gold. Stater.
   Obverse: Similar.
   Reverse: Similar, below, monogram, and in the exergue, an ear of grain.
6. Philip II. Silver. Tetradrachm.
   Obverse: Laureate head of Zeus, right.
   Reverse: King on horseback wearing kausia and mantle, right hand raised, to the left.
7. Philip II. Silver. Tetradrachm.
   Obverse: Similar.
   Reverse: Similar.
8. Philip II. Silver. Tetradrachm.
   Obverse: Laureate head of Zeus, to the left.
   Reverse: Youthful horseman with palm branch, right. Bee.
9. Philip II. Silver. Tetradrachm.
   Obverse: Laureate head of Zeus, to the right.
   Reverse: Similar to No. 8. Bunch of grapes.
10. Philip II. Silver. Tetradrachm.
    Obverse: Similar.
    Reverse: Similar, vase in form of a janiform head.
11. Alexander III. Gold. Stater.
    Obverse: Head of Athena in Corinthian helmet. On the bowl, a serpent.
    Reverse: Nike with stylis and wreath. Trident and monogram.
12. Alexander III. Gold. Stater.
    Obverse: Similar.
    Reverse: Similar. Joined foreparts of two horses.
13. Alexander III. Gold. Distater.
    Obverse: Similar.
    Reverse: Similar. Youthful figure with outstretched arms.
14. Alexander III. Gold. Stater.
    Obverse: Similar.
    Reverse: Similar. Cantherus.
15. Alexander III. Gold. Stater.
    Obverse: Similar.
    Reverse: Similar. Pegasus and monogram.
16. Alexander III. Silver. Tetradrachm.
    Obverse: Head of Heracles.
    Reverse: Zeus enthroned holding eagle and sceptre. Forepart of ram.
17. Alexander III. Silver. Tetradrachm.
    Obverse: Similar.
    Reverse: Similar. Athena with two torches.
18. Alexander III. Silver. Tetradrachm.
    Obverse: Similar.
    Reverse: Similar. Dolphin and monogram.
19. Alexander III. Silver. Tetradrachm.
    Obverse: Similar.
    Reverse: Similar. Monogram.

20. Alexander III. Silver. Tetradrachm.
    Obverse: Similar.
    Reverse: Similar. Facing lion's mask and monogram.

56. 1. Philip III. Gold. Stater. 186
    Obverse: Head of Athena in Corinthian helmet. On the bowl, a serpent.
    Reverse: Nike with stylis and wreath.

2. Philip III. Gold. Stater.
    Obverse: Similar.
    Reverse: Similar.

3. Philip III. Gold. Stater.
    Obverse: Similar.
    Reverse: Similar.

4. Philip III. Gold. Stater.
    Obverse: Similar.
    Reverse: Similar.

5. Seleucus I. Gold. Stater.
    Obverse: Similar. On the bowl, a griffin.
    Reverse: Similar. Barbaric issue.

6. Philip III. Silver. Tetradrachm.
    Obverse: Head of Heracles.
    Reverse: Zeus enthroned holding eagle and sceptre. The king's name.

7. Philip III. Silver. Tetradrachm.
    Obverse: Similar.
    Reverse: Similar.

8. Philip III. Silver. Tetradrachm.
    Obverse: Similar.
    Reverse: Similar.

9. Seleucus I. Silver. Tetradrachm.
    Obverse: Similar.
    Reverse: Similar but with the name of Seleucus.

10. Seleucus I. Silver. Tetradrachm.
    Obverse: Similar.
    Reverse: Similar.

11. Lysimachus. Gold. Stater.
    Obverse: Head of Athena in Corinthian helmet. Serpent on the bowl.
    Reverse: Nike with stylis and wreath. Forepart of lion.

12. Lysimachus. Gold. Stater.
    Obverse: Head of deified Alexander III.
    Reverse: Athena seated with spear and shield, holding Nike.

13. Lysimachus. Gold. Stater.
    Obverse: Similar.
    Reverse: Similar.

14. Lysimachus. Gold. Stater.
    Obverse: Similar.
    Reverse: Similar. In the exergue, a trident.

15. Demetrius Poliorcetes. Gold. Stater.
    Obverse: Head of Athena wearing a Corinthian helmet. On the bowl, a serpent.
    Reverse: Nike with stylis and a wreath and the name of the king.

Page

16. Lysimachus. Silver. Tetradrachm.
    Obverse: Head of deified Alexander III.
    Reverse: Athena seated with spear and shield, holding Nike. Lion mask in profile.
17. Lysimachus. Silver. Tetradrachm.
    Obverse: Similar.
    Reverse: Similar.
18. Lysimachus. Silver. Tetradrachm.
    Obverse: Similar.
    Reverse: Similar.
19. Lysimachus. Silver. Tetradrachm.
    Obverse: Similar.
    Reverse: Similar.
20. Lysimachus. Silver. Tetradrachm.
    Obverse: Similar.
    Reverse: Similar.

57. 1. Eumenes I. Silver. Tetradrachm.   187
    Obverse: Laureate head of Philetaerus.
    Reverse: Athena seated, with shield and spear. Bow.
2. Attalus I. Silver. Tetradrachm.
    Obverse: Similar.
    Reverse: Similar, but the shield is behind Athena and she is crowning the name in front of her. Ivy leaf and A.
3. Attalus I. Silver. Tetradrachm.
    Obverse: Similar.
    Reverse: Similar.
4. Attalus I. Silver. Tetradrachm.
    Obverse: Similar.
    Reverse: Similar.
5. Attalus I. Silver. Tetradrachm.
    Obverse: Similar.
    Reverse: Similar.
6. Cistophoric Tetradrachm. Sardes. Silver.
    Obverse: Cista Mystica with serpent, all in ivy wreath.
    Reverse: Bow in case with serpents. Zeus holding an eagle.
7. Cistophoric Tetradrachm. Pergamum. Silver.
    Obverse: Similar.
    Reverse: Similar. Head of Medusa.
8. Cistophoric Tetradrachm. Ephesus. Silver.
    Obverse: Similar.
    Reverse: Similar. Bust of Ephesian Artemis.
9. Cistophoric Tetradrachm. Apamea. Silver.
    Obverse: Similar.
    Reverse: Similar. Omphalos.
10. Cistophoric Tetradrachm. Tralles. Silver.
    Obverse: Similar.
    Reverse: Similar. Standing figure.
11. Byzantium. Silver. Tetradrachm.
    Obverse: Heifer, below dolphin.
    Reverse: Incuse square with heavy granulations.

12. Byzantium. Silver. Tetradrachm.
    Obverse: Veiled head of Demeter.
    Reverse: Poseidon seated on a rock, holding trident and aplustre.
13. Byzantium. Silver. Tetradrachm.
    Obverse: Similar.
    Reverse: Similar.
14. Byzantium. Silver. Tetradrachm.
    Obverse: Similar.
    Reverse: Similar.
15. Calchedon. Silver. Tetradrachm.
    Obverse: Bull standing on an ear of corn.
    Reverse: Incuse square with heavy granulations.
16. Demetrius Poliorcetes. Silver. Tetradrachm.
    Obverse: Diademed and horned head of Demetrius.
    Reverse: Poseidon seated on rock, holding aplustre and trident.
17. Demetrius Poliorcetes. Silver. Tetradrachm.
    Obverse: Similar.
    Reverse: Poseidon with trident, standing with right foot on rock.
18. Demetrius Poliorcetes. Silver. Tetradrachm.
    Obverse: Similar.
    Reverse: Similar.
19. Demetrius Poliorcetes. Silver. Tetradrachm.
    Obverse: Similar.
    Reverse: Similar.
20. Demetrius Poliorcetes. Silver. Tetradrachm.
    Obverse: Nike with trumpet and stylis standing on prow.
    Reverse: Poseidon brandishing trident, chlamys on left arm.

58. *1 through 10* Antigonus Gonatas. Silver. Tetradrachm.   188
    Obverse: Macedonian shield; in center, head of Pan with pedium at shoulder.
    Reverse: Athena Alkis; to the left a Macedonian helmet; to the right, a monogram.
    11 through 20 Antigonus Doson. Silver. Tetradrachm.
    Obverse: Head of Poseidon with wreath of seaweed.
    Reverse: Apollo, holding strung bow, seated on prow. The name of the king and a monogram.

59. 1. Perseus. Silver. Tetradrachm.   189
    Obverse: Diademed head of Perseus.
    Reverse: Eagle on fulmen within an oak wreath.
   2. Perseus. Silver. Tetradrachm.
    Obverse: Similar.
    Reverse: Similar.
   3. Perseus. Silver. Tetradrachm.
    Obverse: Similar.
    Reverse: Similar.
   4. Philip V. Silver. Tetradrachm.
    Obverse: Diademed head of Philip.
    Reverse: Athena Alkis, the king's name and monograms.
   5. Philip Andriscus. Silver. Tetradrachm.
    Obverse: Macedonian shield; in center, head of Andriscus as Perseus, wearing winged cap with griffin crest, harpa at shoulder.
    Reverse: Club in oak wreath and the king's name.

		Page

6. *Prusius I. Silver. Tetradrachm.*
   Obverse: Diademed head of Prusius.
   Reverse: Zeus with sceptre and wreath. The king's name. Fulmen.
7. *Prusius I. Silver. Tetradrachm.*
   Obverse: Similar.
   Reverse: Similar.
8. *Prusius I. Silver. Tetradrachm.*
   Obverse: Similar.
   Reverse: Similar.
9. *Nicomedes III. Silver. Tetradrachm.*
   Obverse: Diademed head of Nicomedes.
   Reverse: Zeus with sceptre and wreath. Eagle on fulmen.
10. *Nicomedes IV. Silver. Tetradrachm.*
    Obverse: Similar.
    Reverse: Similar.
11. *Tenedos. Silver. Tetradrachm.*
    Obverse: Janiform head, male and female.
    Reverse: Double ax, grapes, the discouri helmets, all within a laurel wreath.
12. *Aegae. Silver. Tetradrachm.*
    Obverse: Laureate head of Apollo; at shoulder, bow and quiver.
    Reverse: Zeus with sceptre and eagle, monogram, all within an oak wreath.
13. *Cyme. Silver. Tetradrachm.*
    Obverse: Head of Amazon Cyme, hair bound with ribbon.
    Reverse: Bridled horse with foreleg raised; below, one-handled cup; all in a laurel wreath.
14. *Myrina. Silver. Tetradrachm.*
    Obverse: Laureate and filleted head of Apollo.
    Reverse: Apollo holding patera and filleted laurel branch. Omphalos and amphora, all in a laurel wreath.
15. *Heracleia. Silver. Tetradrachm.*
    Obverse: Head of Athena in crested Athenian helmet adorned with the foreparts of horses, a flying Pegasus.
    Reverse: Club in oak wreath, owl and monograms and name.

60. *1* through *5*. Athens. Silver. Tetradrachms. Sixth century B.C.   190
    Obverse: Head of Athena in Attic helmet.
    Reverse: Owl, right; to left, olive spray.
    6 through *10*. Athens. Silver. Tetradrachms. Early fifth-century B.C.
    Obverse: Head of Athena in Attic helmet, with three olive leaves on helmet.
    Reverse: Owl, right; to left, olive spray and crescent.
    11 through *15*. Silver. Tetradrachms. Mid fifth century B.C.
    Obverse: Head of Athena in Attic helmet, as in preceding.
    Reverse: As in preceding.
    16 through *18*. Athens. Silver. Tetradrachms. Late fifth century B.C.
    Obverse: Similar to preceding.
    Reverse: Similar to preceding.
    19. Athens. Silver. Tetradrachm. Ancient Anatolian imitation.
    Obverse: Similar.
    Reverse: Owl to left.

20. Athens. Silver. Tetradrachm. Ancient Babylonic imitation.
Obverse: Similar.
Reverse: Similar, except ethnic replaced by four other letters.

61. 1. Smyrna. Silver. Tetradrachm. 191
Obverse: Turreted head of Cybele.
Reverse: Name of city in oak wreath.
2. Magnesia. Silver. Tetradrachm.
Obverse: Head of Artemis wearing stephanus; at shoulder, bow and quiver.
Reverse: Apollo standing on maeander, holding a branch and leaning on a tripod, all in the laurel wreath.
3. Sinope. Silver. Tetradrachm.
Obverse: Head of Sinope wearing turreted crown.
Reverse: Apollo on omphalos, holding lyre and plectrum.
Obverse: Countermarked, head of Athena.
Reverse: Countermarked, head of Heracles.
4. Pontus: Mithridates VI. Silver. Tetradrachm.
Obverse: Diademed head of Mithridates.
Reverse: Name of king, stag feeding, star and crescent all in an ivy wreath.
5. Similar, but different die and month.
6. Lycia. Zamu. Silver. Stater.
Obverse: Facing lion's scalp.
Reverse: Tresceles and, in the field, small tresceles.
7. Lycia. Mithrapata. Silver. Stater.
Obverse: Head and foreleg of lion.
Reverse: Name. Head of Mithrapata. Tresceles.
8. Lycia. Mithrapata. Silver. Stater.
Obverse: Facing lion's scalp; below, tresceles.
Reverse: Similar to No.7.
9. Lycia. Mithrapata. Silver. Stater.
Obverse: Facing lion's scalp.
Reverse: Tresceles. Barley grain.
10. Lycia. Parikla. Silver. Stater.
Obverse: Facing head of Parikla.
Reverse: Helmeted warrior with spear and shield. Tresceles.
11. Pamphylia: Aspendus. Silver. Stater.
Obverse: Two wrestlers.
Reverse: Slinger. Tresceles.
12. Pamphylia: Aspendus. Silver. Stater.
Obverse: Two wrestlers, knuckle bone.
Reverse: Slinger. Tresceles.
13. Pamphylia: Aspendus. Silver. Stater.
Obverse: Two wrestlers.
Reverse: Slinger. Eros. Countermarked: bull.
14. Pamphylia: Aspendus. Silver. Stater.
Obverse: Two wrestlers.
Reverse: Slinger. Tresceles. Eagle.
15. Pamphylia: Aspendus. Silver. Stater.
Obverse: Two wrestlers.
Reverse: Slinger. Tresceles. Club.

16. Cilicia. Celenderis. Silver. Stater.
   Obverse: Horseman holding whip.
   Reverse: Goat kneeling, head reverted.
17. Cilicia. Celenderis. Silver. Stater.
   Obverse: Horseman holding whip.
   Reverse: Goat kneeling, head reverted.
18. Cilicia. Nagidus. Silver. Stater.
   Obverse: Aphrodite seated on throne with low back, holding phial; to left Eros flying with wreath; below throne, mouse.
   Reverse: Dionysus holding thyrsus and vine branch.
19. Cilicia. Tarsus. Pharnabazus. Silver. Stater.
   Obverse: Baaltars seated, holding sceptre.
   Reverse: Helmeted male head (Ares or a Satrap).
20. Cilicia. Tarsus. Silver. Stater.
   Obverse: Baaltars seated, holding sceptre.
   Reverse: Helmeted male head (Ares or a Satrap).

62. 1. Cilicia. Tarsus. Pharnabazus. Silver. Stater.   192
   Obverse: Female head facing.
   Reverse: Helmeted male head (Ares or a Satrap).
2. Cilicia. Tarsus. Datames. Silver. Stater.
   Obverse: Female head facing.
   Reverse: Helmeted male head (Ares or a Satrap) to right.
3. Similar.
4. Similar. Reverse with head to left.
5. Similar.
6. Cilicia. Tarsus. Datames. Silver. Stater.
   Obverse: Baaltars seated, holding in right hand eagle-headed sceptre and in the left an ear of grain and bunch of grapes; to the right, thymiaterion; all in a circle with projections resembling battlements.
   Reverse: Ana, left and Datames, right, standing facing with thymiaterion between them, all within a linear square with dots along top and sides.
7. Cilicia. Tarsus. Datames. Silver. Stater.
   Obverse: Similar to No. 6.
   Reverse: Datames in satrapal dress seated right, holding an arrow in both hands. Winged sun disk. Bow.
8. Cilicia. Tarsus. Mazaeus. Silver. Stater.
   Obverse: Baaltars seated, holding in left hand lotus-headed sceptre and in the right an eagle; ear of grain and bunch of grapes.
   Reverse: Lion attacking bull.
9. Cilicia. Tarsus. Mazaeus. Silver. Stater.
   Obverse: Baaltars seated holding eagle-headed sceptre. To the left, ear of grain and a bunch of grapes.
   Reverse: Two lines of walls each with four towers, one above the other; lion attacking a bull.
10. Cilicia. Tarsus. Mazaeus. Silver. Stater.
   Obverse: Baaltars seated holding a lotus-headed sceptre; to the left a bunch of grapes, to the right, an ivy leaf.
   Reverse: Facing head of Athena in crested Attic helmet.

11. Rhodes. Silver. Tetradrachm.
    Obverse: Facing head of Helios.
    Reverse: Rose. Dolphin.
12. Rhodes. Silver. Tetradrachm.
    Obverse: Facing head of Helios.
    Reverse: Rose.
13. Rhodes. Silver. Tetradrachm.
    Obverse: Facing head of Helios, radiate.
    Reverse: Rose. Bud. Acrostolium.
14. Caria. Mausolus. Silver. Tetradrachm.
    Obverse: Facing head of Helios.
    Reverse: Zeus Labrandius with spear and double ax. Wreath.
15. Caria. Hidrieus. Silver. Tetradrachm.
    Obverse: Facing head of Helios.
    Reverse: Zeus Labrandius with spear and double ax.
16. Samos. Silver. Tetradrachm.
    Obverse: Lion's scalp, facing.
    Reverse: Head and neck of bull.
17. Magnesia. Silver. Tridrachm.
    Obverse: Mounted spearman.
    Reverse: Humped bull.
18. Aenus. Silver. Tetradrachm.
    Obverse: Head of Hermes, facing.
    Reverse: Goat, standing.
19. Apollonia Pontica. Silver. Tetradrachm.
    Obverse: Laureate head of Apollo.
    Reverse: Anchor. Crayfish.
20. Ionia. Colophon. Silver. Drachm.
    Obverse: Laureate head of Apollo.
    Reverse: Lyre.

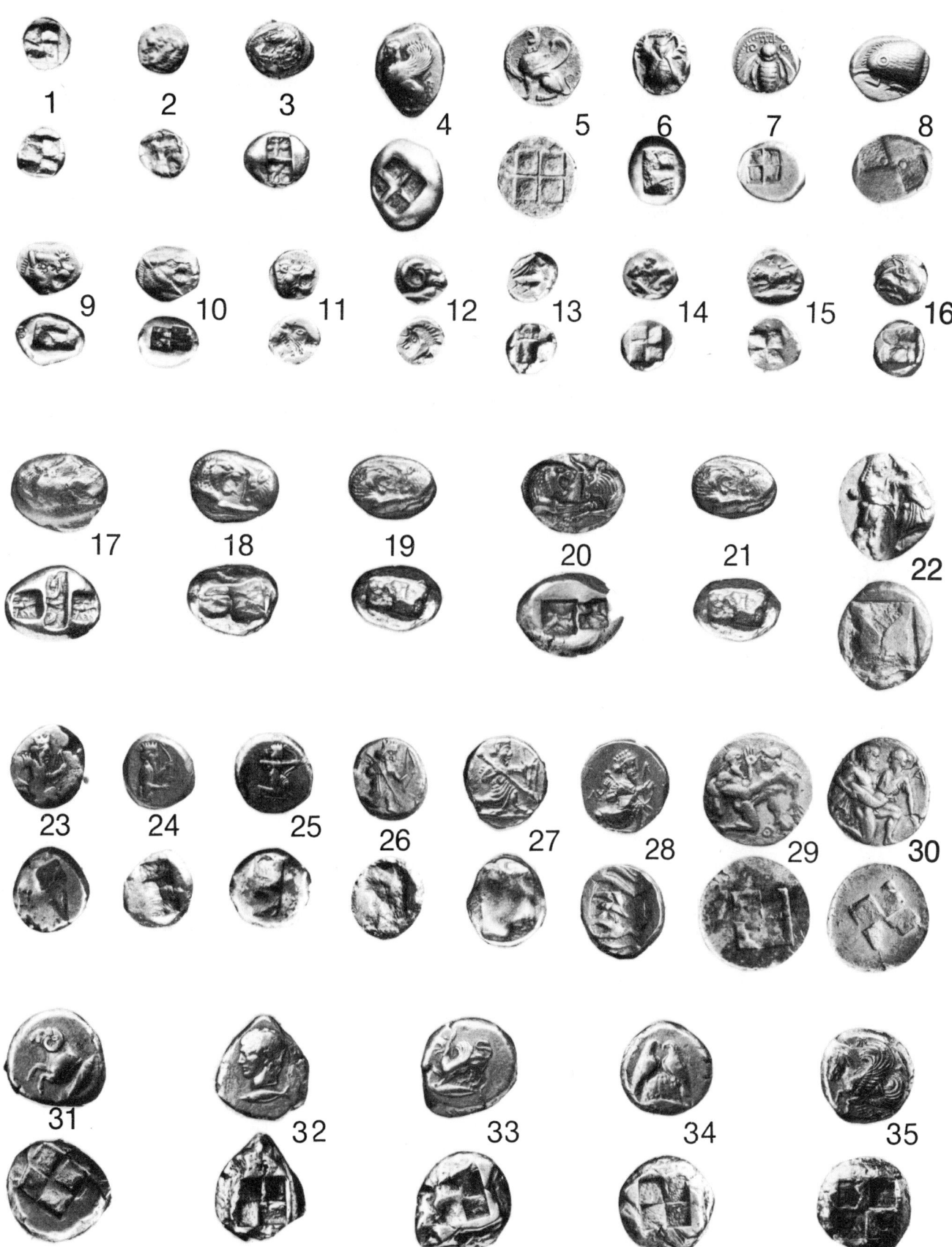

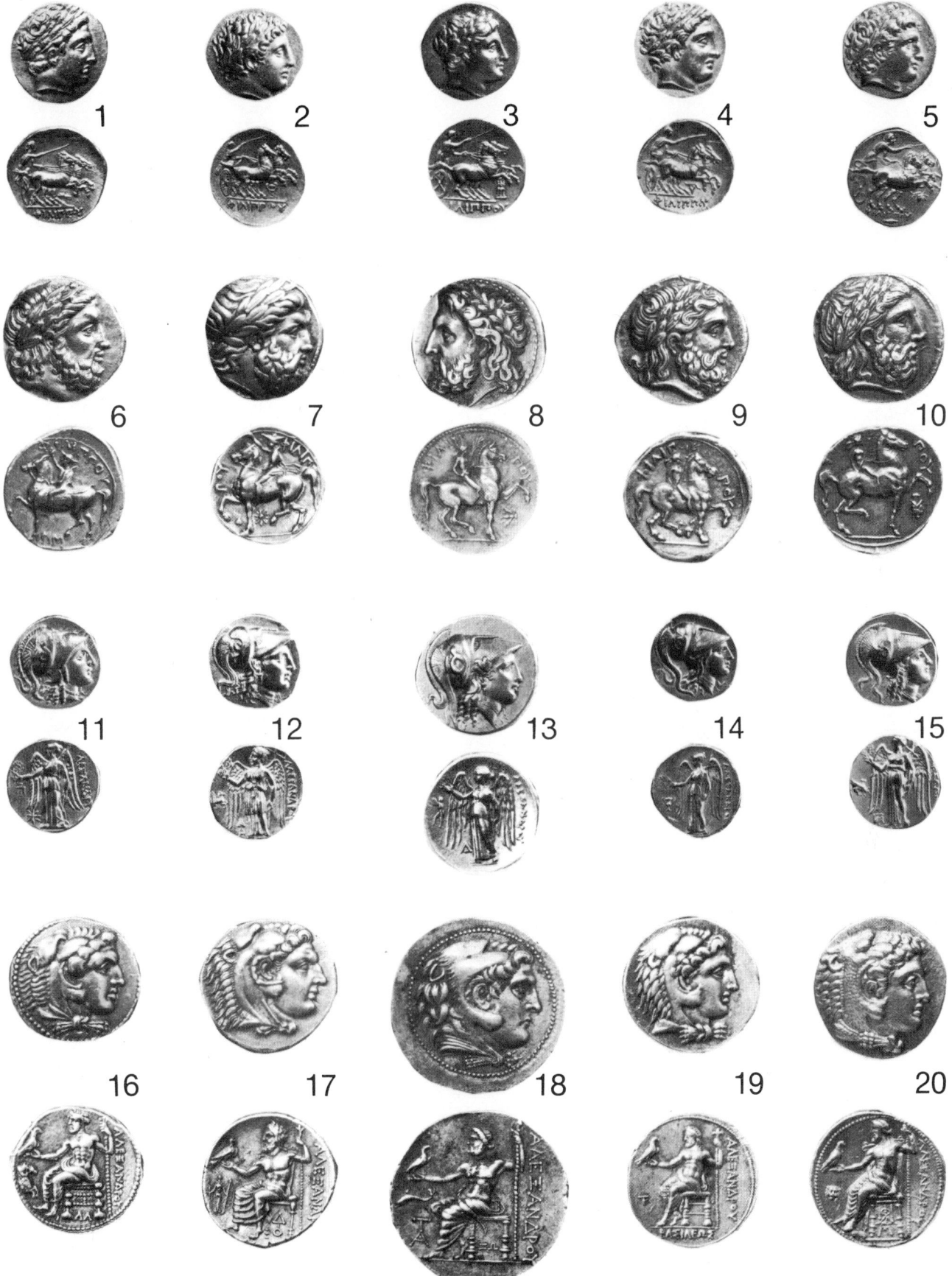

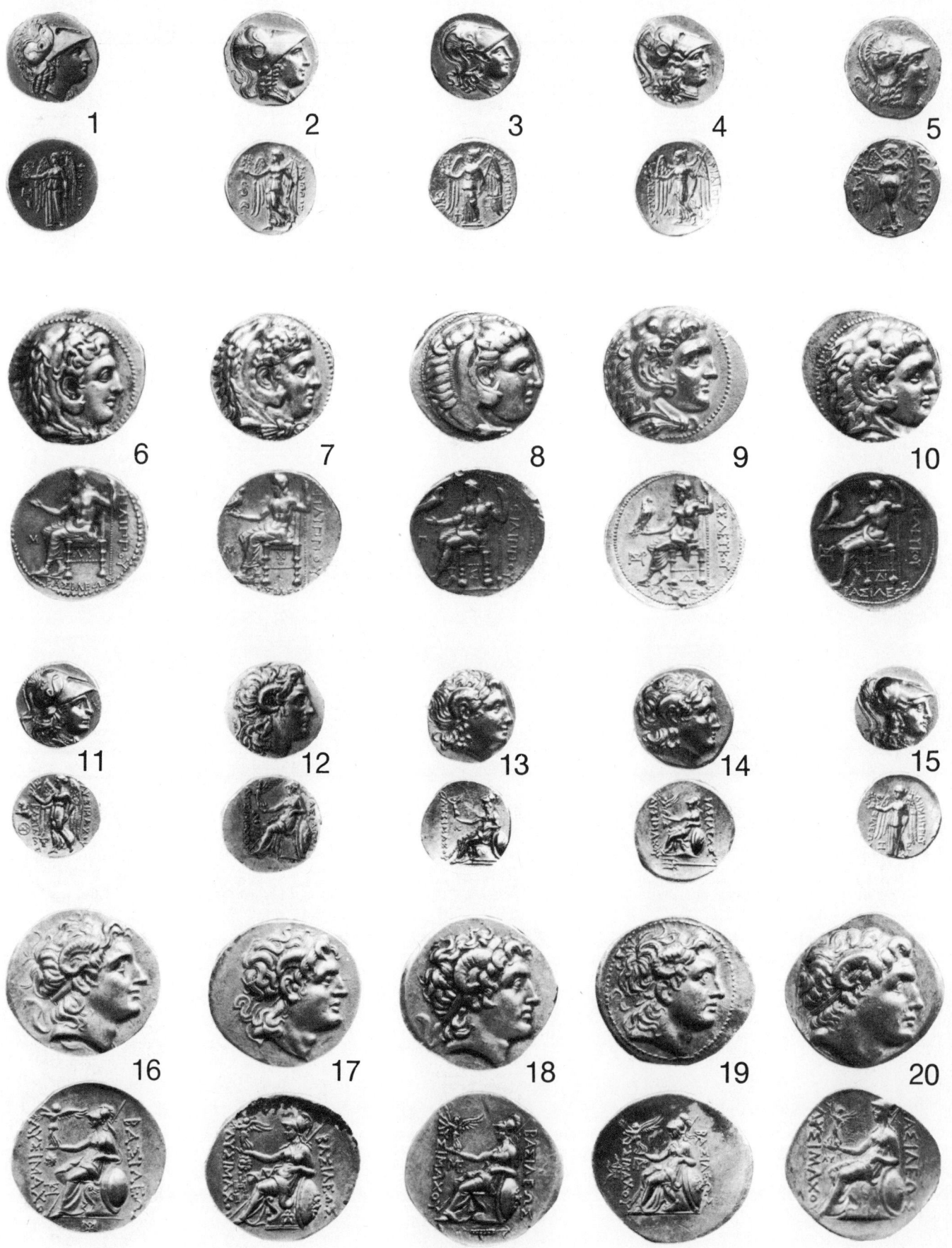

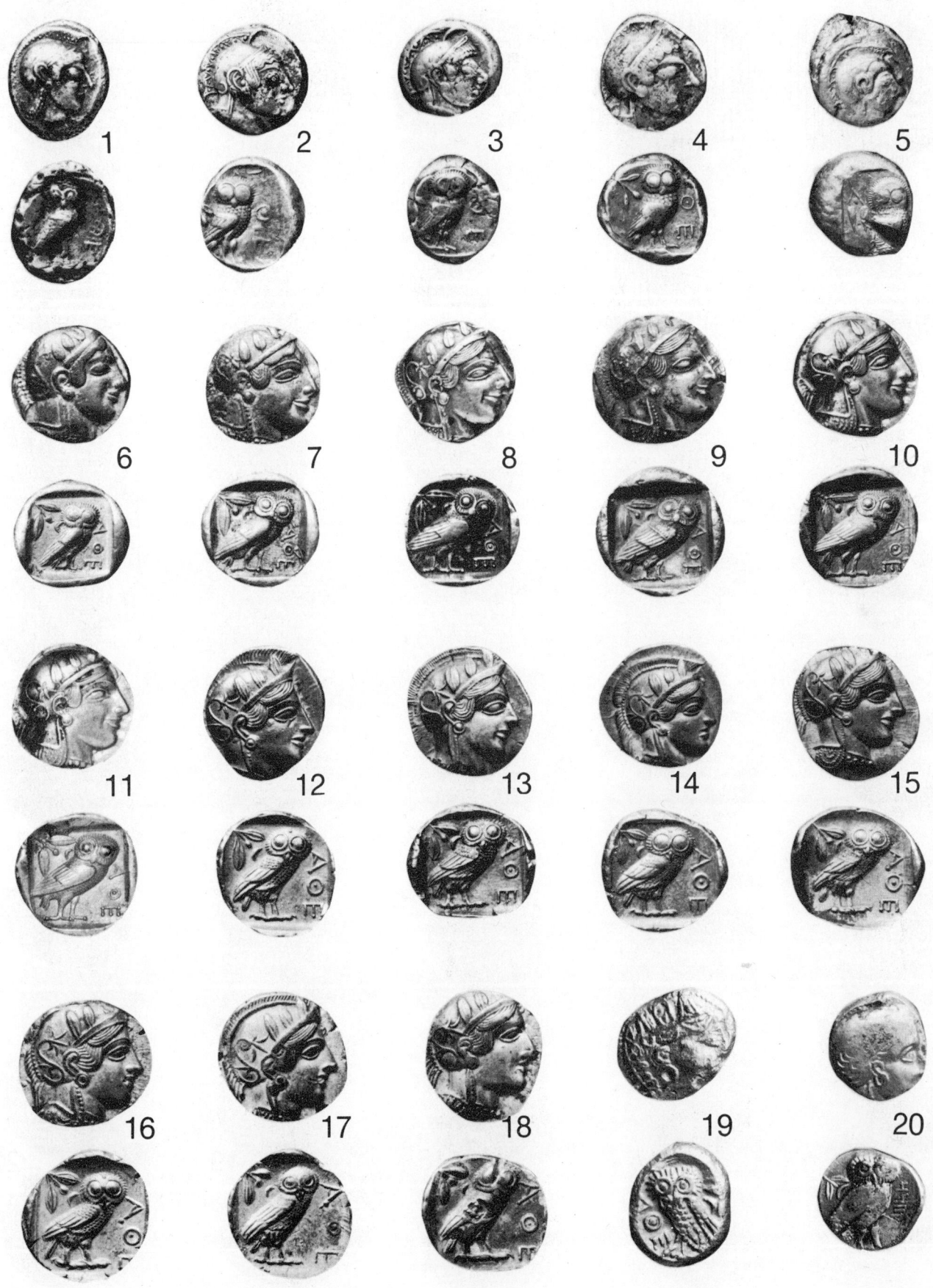